A YEAR WITH EMERSON

A YEAR WITH
EMERSON

A DAYBOOK

selected & edited by

Richard Grossman

with engravings by
Barry Moser

David R. Godine · *Publisher*

BOSTON

First published in 2003 by
David R. Godine, Publisher
Post Office Box 450
Jaffrey, New Hampshire 03452
www.godine.com

LIBRARY OF CONGRESS CATALOGING-IN-PUBLICATION DATA

Emerson, Ralph Waldo, 1803–1882
A year with Emerson : A daybook / selected and edited by
Richard Grossman ; engravings by Barry Moser. — 1st. ed.
p.   cm.
ISBN-13: 978-1-56792-298-1 (PBK. : ALK. PAPER)
ISBN-10: 1-56792-298-8 (PBK. : ALK. PAPER)
1. Emerson, Ralph Waldo, 1803-1882—Quotations. I.
Grossman, Richard L. (Richard Lee), 1921– II. Title.
PS1603.G76 2005
818'.302—DC22
2005016134

First Softcover Edition
PRINTED IN THE UNITED STATES OF AMERICA

In memory of Henry Geiger

1909—1989

Socrates lived again in Los Angeles

CONTENTS

Preface · · · · · *ix*

A Note to the Reader · *xv*

January · · · · · *1*

February · · · · *21*

March · · · · · *39*

April · · · · · · *57*

May · · · · · · *73*

June · · · · · · *95*

July · · · · · · *113*

August · · · · *133*

September · · *151*

October · · · · *169*

November · · *189*

December · · · *209*

Additional Reading · *229*

Acknowledgments · *231*

PREFACE

THIS BOOK is an invitation to spend time with one of the most provocative teachers who ever lived. Although Ralph Waldo Emerson has more often been called a poet, essayist, lecturer, or philosopher, when he wasn't being lionized as "The George Washington of American Literature" or "The Isaiah of His Age," his work and life were dedicated to the mission of teaching.

Not teaching with the emphasis on content, or data, not teaching us what to think, certainly not how to think, but rather teaching us how vital it is *to* think. He did suggest some of the matters we as thinkers might consider: Is a scientific view of the world compatible with moral beliefs and spiritual appetites? Is matter "blind" or is everything in nature evolving into consciousness? Is there a personal God, or is God present throughout the universe? Can we, as the Idealists do, "insist on the power of thought and will, on inspiration, on miracles, on individual culture?" Can we reconcile the apparent conflict between our membership in society and our need for solitude?

All these issues and more Emerson explored in a long life that was marred by early struggle of the most difficult kind. His first twenty-five years, which began on May 25th, 1803, were spent in good part trying simply to survive physically. His family was genetically prone to the "consumption" (tuberculosis) of his time; he lost three of his four brothers to the disease (as well as his beloved first wife,

Ellen Tucker, who died eighteen months after they married). He himself, in his early twenties, needed to go South to "strengthen his lungs" and regain his energy. Regain it he did, displaying an immense vigor over the years, crossing the Mississippi River again and again on the winter ice in order to keep his annual lecture appearances in the West, or walking forty miles to Worcester, worrying not about his legs but about how few persons were on the road to pay the turnpike tolls.

Despite these feats, Emerson worried about his health from his teens onward and must have presented himself as delicate because, as he was amused to note, his friends often greeted him with the query, "Aren't you just a little thinner than when last I saw you?" He was a slender man, probably never carrying more than 150 pounds on his almost six-foot frame, but if his shoulders sloped and he appeared frail it was his strong poetic face that most people noticed. As his friend and biographer, Oliver Wendell Holmes, said, "His expression was calm, sedate, kindly; his manner noble and gracious." And then there was his voice, a resonant, almost hypnotic baritone that seemed to be destiny's gift to the man who became the foremost lecturer of this time. As a persistent writer he produced more than fifty volumes of poems, addresses, hymns, lectures, and letters that have inspired generations of readers all over the world. To all his work he brought a distinctly American perspective, an attitude that more than tipped its hat to the legacies of our English and Continental heritages, but at the same time sounded a note of rugged, independent, autonomous Americanism. For this reason he can be also be seen as the Johnny Appleseed of nineteenth-century American culture and must be given credit for inspiring, and in many cases sponsoring, some of the most important and uniquely American writers and thinkers we have produced, from Walt Whitman to Melville, from Thoreau to Hawthorne, from William James to John Dewey. Even twentieth-century figures like Frank Lloyd Wright, Charles Ives, and Wallace Stevens, in their pragmatism, their preoccupation with the primacy of the senses, their predilection for analogy, and above all, their dedication to individuality and self-reliance, can all be seen as profiting from Emerson's example.

His influence must be recognized, too, in what the religious scholar Diana Eck has called "the 'Easting' of old New England." Introduced to Hindu scriptures by his aunt Mary Moody Emerson in the 1820s, Emerson became deeply involved with Hindu thought throughout the 1830s. He and Thoreau exchanged texts and ideas about Eastern thought, with Thoreau finally acknowledging that "farthest India is nearer to me than Concord " and Emerson paraphrasing the Vedantic texts by declaring, "I can, with a modest aspiring, say 'I am God', by transferring me out of the unclean precincts of my body, my fortunes, my private will. . . ."

But even as we acknowledge his influence in so many areas and on so many people we come across a contradiction: Emerson had no "disciples" – as such. He himself boasted that they "[disciples] would interrupt and encumber me. . . . I have no school follower. I should account it a measure of the impurity of insight, if [what I said] did not create independence." There we have the essence of his commitment, his mission not to "bring men to him, but to themselves."

So his work does not become an *œuvre* of Emersonian philosophy, or Emersonian political theory or Emersonian economic policy, but rather the individual voice of one man trying to help us elicit the philosopher, the political theorist, the economic thinker in us. Like Lao-Tse in the *Tao Te Ching*, which has been called 2,500 words against language, Emerson preached against preaching and urged teachers not to teach, but to make learning possible. This avoidance of any formal system, this embrace of contradiction, this deeply held belief in the never-ending undulation of nature and events, this Solomonic conviction that "all things are double one against the other" – all these have led to criticisms of Emerson as "diffuse," "hazy," "dreamy," "unrealistic," and to be sure, he is not always the opposite of these – "focused," "sharp," "practical," and "hard-headed." But throughout all his work he is a poet, and poets have been charged with having visions for us who cannot see, and imagining for us worlds we cannot fathom on our own. And inevitably, his spirit comes through to us, whether in his spoken or written words. He achieves his goal of bringing us to ourselves, his presence resonating in us as it did in such contemporaries as the poet James Russell Lowell in the 1800s:

Behind each word we divine the force of a noble character, the weight of a large capital of thinking and being. We do not go to hear what Emerson says so much as to hear Emerson. . . . If asked what was left? What we carry home? . . . We might have asked in return what one brought away from a symphony of Beethoven?

When reading Emerson, we are well advised to listen to

Lewis Mumford, the great twentieth-century cultural and literary critic, who said, "The way to approach the richness and amplitude of Emerson's mind is to follow his own example in drawing sustenance and energy from the writing of other men; not to read him too conscientiously and consecutively, but to dip into him frequently, almost at random, to find precisely the stimulus or counter-statement, or even the irritation, that perhaps only he could give." In seeing how rewarding Emerson can be, even in small doses, Mumford may be reflecting Emerson's own awareness of his habit of using his journals as a "savings bank," a treasury of his own inner thoughts and feelings which, when he explored and expanded them, formed the heart of his essays, his poems, his lectures – and ultimately his books. One can imagine that he might bless the idea that he be read in short passages from his voluminous writing, with the tone varying from the romantic to the mystical to the mundane, but the substance always relating to his ambition to be Man Thinking. Often, as we read, we may share the experience of Emerson's neighbor, Nathaniel Hawthorne,

It was good to meet him in the wood-paths or sometimes on our avenue with that pure intellectual gleam diffusing about his presence like the garment of a shining one, and he, so great, so simple, so without pretension, encountering each man alive as if expecting to receive more than he would impart. . . . It was impossible to dwell in his vicinity without inhaling more or less the mountain atmosphere of his lofty thought.

A NOTE TO THE READER

In his earliest journals, Emerson wrote, "I confine my ambition to true reporting. I write anecdotes of the intellect, a sort of *Farmer's Almanac* of mental moods." Clearly he far exceeded this modest goal, but perhaps his reference to an "almanac" might be taken as a tacit endorsement of the conception and arrangement of this modest book, which was conceived as a celebration of the man and his work during the year of his bicentennial.

Because the year 2003 will see so many events marking the 200th anniversary of Emerson's birth – and perhaps because I have been reading short excerpts from Emerson daily for over forty years – I was moved to organize this book as a kind of narrative calendar, with one entry for every day in the year. Many of these entries were actually written or spoken by him on the date of the selection. But a prolific and thoughtful man who lives for seventy-nine years has many creative and exciting February 21sts or June 26ths, so it was not always possible to adhere strictly to a precise "almanac" format. Furthermore, Emerson's love for the natural world was such that he wrote about it constantly, and his observations of nature's seasonal riches are too good to miss; hence, many such observations demanded to be given a day appropriate to the weather, and brilliant speeches or essays or poems that might have been written on the date in question had to find a place somewhere in the neighborhood of when they were created.

But the whole year is spent with Emerson, who, as his biographer Robert Richardson, has said, "is as alive, as pertinent now as he was in his lifetime. We have only to reach out for the gifts which Emerson, like a new god on a new day, offers us. . . ."

·JANUARY·

1 *On January 1, 1863, the day the Emancipation Proclamation went into effect, Boston held a "Jubilee Concert." For the occasion Emerson wrote his "Boston Hymn," and a later two of the twenty-two stanzas brought the crowd — including some former slaves — to their feet, cheering wildly and singing his words at the top of their lungs.*

> To-day unbind the captive
> So only are ye unbound
> Lift up a people from the dust,
> Trump of their rescue, sound!

> Pay ransom to the owner
> And fill the bag to the brim
> Who is the owner? The slave is owner,
> And ever was. Pay him.

2 *Even in one of his most famous passages extolling the virtues of books, Emerson finds an opportunity again to sound the clarion call to independence and autonomy.*

Books are the best things well used; abused, among the worst. What is the right use? What is the one end which all means go to affect? They are for nothing but to inspire. I had better never see a book than to be warped by its attraction clean out of my own orbit, and made a satellite instead of a system. The one thing in the world, of value, is the active soul. This every man is entitled to, this every man contains within him, although in almost all men obstructed and unborn. The soul active sees absolute truth and utters truth, or creates. In this action it is genius; not the privilege of here and there a favorite, but the sound estate of every man. In its essence it is progressive.

3 *Written on shipboard as he was sailing near Gibraltar in January 1833.*

If the sea teaches any lesson, it thunders this through the throat of all its winds, "That there is no knowledge that is not valuable." How I envied my fellow passenger who yesterday had knowledge and nerve enough to prescribe for the sailor's sore throat and this morning to bleed him. In this little balloon of ours, so far from the human family and their sages and colleges and manufactories, every accomplishment, every natural or acquired talent, every piece of information is some time in request.

4

Honor is venerable to us because it is no ephemeris. It is always ancient virtue. We worship it today because it is not of to-day. We love and pay it homage, not because it is a trap for our love and homage, but is self-dependent, self-derived, and therefore of an old immaculate pedigree, even if shown in a young person.

5 *A provocative thought – at least in his time – emerges from the mind of an ordained minister.*

Truth; Realism; Are you not scared by seeing that the Gypsies are more attractive to us than the Apostles? For though we love goodness and not stealing, yet we also love freedom and not preaching.

6 *Although he is only twenty-one, Emerson is already showing signs of what will be an almost total abandonment of his religious background. The aunt he speaks of is Mary Moody Emerson, his father's sister, who was one of the great influences on him all his life, though they disagreed violently on many subjects.*

It is my own humor to despise pedigree. I was educated to prize it. The kind Aunt whose cares instructed my youth (and whom may God reward), told me oft the virtues of her and mine ancestors. They have been clergymen for many generations, and the piety of all and the eloquence of many is yet praised in the Churches. But the dead sleep in their moonless night; my business is with the living.

7 *Emerson counts birthdays – not his own, but that of the nation, and he finds it still young at eighty-two. (He was only fifty-five at the time of this calculation in his journals.)*

> 1858
> 1776
> ———
> 82 years count the age of the Union, and

yet they say the nation is old and infirm as a man is with those years. Now a building is not in its prime until after 500 years. Nor should a nation be; and we aged at 80!

8 *Even at the age of fifteen Emerson realized that his letters would be read by others than the people to whom they were addressed, and he tells his brother about how he plans to handle this responsibility.*

Now to tell you the truth there are three or four different moods in which I write to three or four different persons; & in the following order. When I think I should like to write a letter & yet feel sufficiently sober to keep all my nonsense down, then I begin my letter with 'my dear Mother' but when I think I can write a grammatically correct epistle or anything that I am sure can raise the risible muscles of gravity itself *then* I address my fastidious brother – Bachelor – When in a very *compositorial rhetorical* mood, I send to an uncle in the Alibama [*sic*] – and last of all when I want to scribble I know not why, & care not what, & moreover have leisure & rhyme at command, and peradventure want to amuse myself, *then* as *now* the pen flies over the lines to my semi-Andover semi-Boston brother Ned. In short I write to you when I'm in a serio-ludicro-tragico-comico miscellany of feelings.

9 *All his life Emerson was wary of those who blow hot and cold at the same time.*

An idealist, if he have the sensibilities and habits of those whom I know, is very ungrateful. He craves every chemical property and every elemental force, loves pure air, water, light, caloric, wheat, flesh, salt, and sugar; the blood coursing in his own veins; and uses the meat he eats to preach against matter as malignant, and to praise mind, which he very hollowly and treacherously serves. Beware of hypocrisy.

10 *Always generous to his friends, Emerson was quick to write the needed letter of recommendation. This*

one is to the Secretary of State, William H. Seward,
on behalf of Mr. Walt Whitman of New York.

Dear Sir,

Mr. Walt Whitman, of New York, writes me, that he wishes to obtain employment in the public service in Washington, & has made, or is about making some application to yourself.

Permit me to say that he is known to me as a man of strong original genius, combining, with marked eccentricities, great powers and valuable traits of character; a self-relying, large-hearted man, much beloved by his friends; entirely patriotic & benevolent in his theory, tastes, & practice. If his writings are in certain points open to criticism, they yet show extraordinary power, and are more deeply American, democratic & in the interests of political liberty, than those of any other poet. He is indeed a child of the people, & their champion.

11   *One of Emerson's central themes, and the bedrock of all philosophies based on a belief in human potentialities, is here used to encourage young ministers-in-training to trust their own inner vision.*

For all our penny-wisdom, for all our self-destroying slavery to habit, it is not to be doubted that all men have sublime thoughts; that all men value the few real hours of life; they love to be heard; they love to be caught up into the vision of principles. We mark with light in the memory the few interviews we have had, in the dreary years of routine and of sin, with souls that made our souls wiser; that spoke what we thought; that told us what we knew; that gave us leave to be what we inly were. Discharge to men the priestly office, and present or absent, you shall be followed with their love as by an angel.

12 *Even sages sometimes lose their wallets, and sometimes they are rescued by friends.*

Dear Mrs Perkins,

I enclose $10, the sum you so kindly lent me, with my best thanks; but am still vexed with clouding your pure hospitality by your sympathy for such an absurd mishap. In the bare chance that the wallet should be picked up by an honest finder, I add, what I believe I told you, that there was no name, – it was a common purplish one, containing the uncounted bills which Mr. Wicker had just given me, & perhaps $25 or 28 more, two or three bills being of the Concord Mass. bank; some postage stamps, & a blank and cheque of the Atlantic Bank, Boston. I do not think of any other means of identification, & I am quite sure none will be wanted. But I am sorry that I did not say to you that I had rather lose it than have it advertised in any manner.

If you're in my neighborhood, it will give me great pleasure to show you my household. One of these days Willie will come to see me on his way to Cambridge, I hope, if Cambridge mends its faults, & deserves the best boys. But the boys of this day, as I told you, seem to me to have a proud future before them. Yours, with kindest regards,

13 *In England in 1848, he observes at firsthand the Sunday evening coexistence of the sacred and the profane.*

In the minster I heard "God Save the King," of Handel. played by Dr. Camidge on the grand organ. It was very great. I thought I had never heard anything so sublime. The music was made for the minster, & the minster for the music. In the choir was service of evening prayer read and chanted. It was strange to hear the whole history of the betrothal of Rebekah and Isaac in the morning of the world read with all the circumstanciality [*sic*] in York Minster, 13 Jan. 1848, to the decorous English audience just fresh from the Times newspaper & their wine, and they listening with all the devotion of national pride. That was binding old & new to some purpose. The reverence for the Scriptures is a powerful element of civilization, for thus has the history of the world been preserved, & is preserved. Every day a chapter of Genesis and a leader in the Times.

14

The great value of biography consists in the perfect sympathy that exists between like minds. Space & time are an absolute nullity to this principle. An action of Luther's that I heartily approve I do adopt also. . . . Socrates, St. Paul, Antoninus, Luther, Milton have lived for us as much as for their contemporaries if by books or by tradition their life & words come to my ear. We recognize with delight a strict likeness between their noblest impulses & our own. We are tried in their trial. By our cordial approval we conquer in their victory. We participate in their act by our thorough understanding of it.

15

This strong-winged sea-gull and striped sheer-water that
you have watched as they skim the waves under our vault,
they are works of art better worth your enthusiasm, mas-
terpieces of Eternal power, strictly eternal because now
active, and ye need not go so far to seek what ye would not
seek at all if it were not within you. Yet welcome and hail!
So sang in my ear the silver-grey mists, and the winds and
the sea said Amen.

16

*Some observers see this poem as offsetting what
Lewis Mumford has called "the shrinking tender-
mindedness of some of his youthful perceptions,"
and it certainly is at odds with Emerson's repeated
rejection of "the yoke of other men's opinions."*

GRACE

How much, preventing God, how much I owe
To the defenses thou hast round me set;
Example, custom, fear, occasion slow,–
These scorned bondmen were my parapet
I dare not peep over this parapet.
The depths of sin to which I had descended,
Had not these me against myself defended.

17

*Emerson is clear about his principles, but he is also
aware of the contradictions between them and some
of his earthly habits.*

The two parties in life are the believers & unbelievers, var-

iously named. The believer is poet, saint, democrat, theo-
crat, free-trade, no-church, no capital punishment, idealist.

The unbeliever supports the church, education, the
fine arts, &c as *amusements.* . . .

But the unbelief is very profound; who can escape it?

I am nominally a believer: yet I hold on to property: I
eat my bread with unbelief. I approve every wild action of
the experimenters. I say what they say concerning celiba-
cy or money or community of goods and my only apolo-
gy for not doing their work is preoccupation of mind. I
have a work of my own which I know I can do with some
success. It would leave that undone if I should undertake
with them and I do not see in myself any vigour equal to
such an enterprise. My Genius loudly calls me to stay where
I am, even with the degradation of owning bankstock and
seeing poor men suffer whilst the Universal Genius apprises me of this disgrace & beckons me to the martyr's &
redeemer's office.

18   *Newspapers reported that this address was delivered in the presence of President Lincoln and some
of his cabinet a few months before the issuing of
the Emancipation Proclamation.*

Emancipation removes the whole objection to union.
Emancipation at one stroke elevates the poor white of the
South, and identifies his interest with that of the Northern
laborer.

Now, in the name of all that is simple and generous,
why should not this great right be done? Why should not
America be capable of a second stroke for the well-being

of the human race, as eighty or ninety years ago she was for the first, – of an affirmative step in the interests of human civility, urged on her, too, not by any romance of sentiment, but by her own extreme perils? It is very certain that the statesman who shall break through the cobwebs of doubt, fear and petty evil that lie in the way, will be greeted by the unanimous links of mankind. . . .

 At the age of sixty-nine he writes a colorful travelogue to his wife about the trip up the Nile that he took with his daughter Ellen.

We enjoy heartily this watery journey, & have spent the last two days in the colossal temples on the two sides of the river here. Every day is clear & hot, the sky rich, the shores lined with palm groves, the birds innumerable, the ibis, the penguin, the hawk & the eagle, with vast flights of geese & ducks & flocks of little birds of sparrow size who fly and in a rolling globe, whirl round & return again every minute. The crocodile is promised to us a little higher up the river but not yet seen. The Nile has daily the appearance of a long lake whose end we are always fast approaching, but the shores separate as we come to them opening new lakes of which we choose the broadest. Egypt is nothing but a long strip of land lined with a rocky desert on either side, & the river brings down each year the mud from the unknown regions in the South to give these wretched ribbon strips three harvests instead of one. The people are negroes in color, & often in the whole head and face, but are called Arabs, speak Arabic, and have excellent forms.

20

Society never advances. It recedes as fast on one side as it gains on the other. It undergoes continual changes; it is barbarous, it is civilized, it is Christianized, it is rich, it is scientific; but this change is not amelioration. For everything that is given, something is taken. Society acquires new arts, and loses old instincts.

21 *Yet again Emerson finds a way to redefine poetry and to express his reverence for it.*

Poetry is the perpetual endeavor to express the spirit of the thing, to pass the brute body, and search the life and reason which causes it to exist; – to see that the object is always flowing away, whilst the spirit or necessity which causes it subsists. Its essential mark is that it betrays in every word instant activity of mind, shown in new uses of every fact and image, – in preternatural quickness or perception of relations. All its words are poems. It is a presence of mind that gives a miraculous command of all means of uttering the thought and feeling of the moment. The poet squanders in an hour the amount of life that would more than furnish the seventy years of the man that stands next to him.

22 *Emerson is fascinated by his dreams, and his exploration of them is much in the spirit of modern psychological interpretation.*

Dreams. I have often experienced, and again last night, in my dreams, the surprise and curiosity of a stranger or indifferent observer to the trait or the motive and information communicated. Thus some refractory youth, of whom I had some guidance or authority, expressed very frankly his dissent and dislike, disliked my way of laughing. I was curious to understand the objection, and endeavored to penetrate and appreciate it, and of course, with the usual misfortune, that when I awoke and attempted to recover the specification, which was remarkable, it was utterly forgotten. But the fact that I, who must be the author of both parts of the dialogue, am thus remote and inquisitive in regard to one part, is ever wonderful.

23 *In an uncharacteristic outburst, Emerson reveals to his journal the conflict he feels between being an intellectual on the one hand and a "naturalist" on the other.*

The child, the infant is a transcendentalist & charms us all. We try to be, & instantly run in debt, lie, steal, commit adultery, go mad, & die. Each practical mistake that we add to our sins, reacts on us, & spoils our tune & temper, steals away all our edge & manhood, & we are eunuchs & women. Narrow & narrower grows the line on which we must walk; deep the gulf on either hand, the man is weary of labor & mere repetition of tasks, & would willingly exchange some of this rude health for some intellectual culture. Instantly we say, how hollow – how white he is, a man of verbs & nouns! God is grown but a noun; & philosophy, spirit, & heaven a grammar exercise. Well, the man of letters takes to the field, & very soon the field enters him, & he grows cloddy and rude. Disgusts on both sides. I hate books, they are an usurpation & impertinence. I cannot once go home to truth & Nature for this perpetual clutter of words & dust of libraries. Yet take me at my word & burn my books &, like poor Petrarch, I might come to insanity for want of this fine wine of the gods.

24 *Emerson makes clear that while he honors the farmer, the scientist, the laborer, he respects, above all, "Man Thinking."*

Not he is great who can alter matter, but he who can alter my state of mind. They are the kings of the world who give the color of their present thought to all nature and all art, and persuade men by the cheerful serenity of their carrying the matter, that this thing which they do is the apple which the ages have desired to pluck, now at last ripe and inviting nations to the harvest. The great man makes the great thing. . . . The day is always his who works in it with serenity and great aims. The unstable estimates of men crowd to him whose mind is filled with a truth, as the heaped waves of the Atlantic follow the moon.

25 *Emerson's lecture, "Man the Reformer," delivered on January 25, 1841, before the Mechanics' Apprentices Library Association, anticipates many sentiments of modern critics of the corporate culture.*

The ways of trade are grown selfish to the borders of theft, and supple to the borders (if not beyond the borders) of fraud. The employments of commerce are not intrinsically unfit for a man, or less genial to his faculties; but these are now in their general course so vitiated by derelictions and abuses at which all connive, that it requires more vigor

and resources than can be expected of every young man
... the general system of our trade ... is a system of self-
ishness; it is not dictated by the high sentiments of human
nature; is not measured by the exact law of reciprocity,
much less by the sentiments of love and heroism, but is a
system of distrust, concealment, of superior keenness, not
of giving but of taking advantage.

 The man who wanted, above all things, to be known as a poet here offers one of his many definitions of what constitutes such an artist.

The breadth of the problem is great, for the poet is representative. He stands among partial man for the complete
man and apprises us not of his wealth, but of the common
wealth. The young man reveres men of genius, because, to
speak truly, they are more himself than he is. They receive
of the soul as he also receives, but they more. ... He is isolated among his contemporaries by truth and by his art,
but with this consolation in his pursuits, that they will
draw all men sooner or later. For all men live by truth and
stand in need of expression. In love, in art, in avarice, in
politics, in labor, in games, we study to utter our painful
secret. The man is only half himself, the other half is his
expression.

Emerson takes another stand against conformity and even singles out Jesus as being prone to it.

For Nature, who abhors mannerism, has set her heart on
breaking up all styles and tricks, and it is so much easier

to do what one has done before than to do a new thing, that there is a perpetual tendency to a set mode. In every conversation, even the highest, there is a certain trick, which may soon be learned by an acute person and then that particular style continued indefinitely. Each man too is a tyrant in tendency, because he would impose his idea on others; and their trick is their natural defence. Jesus would absorb the race; but Tom Paine or the coarsest blasphemer helps humanity by resisting this exuberance of power.

28

Here, we get some idea of how hard Emerson tried to live up to his own standards.

If I should write an honest diary, which should I say? Alas, that life has halfness, shallowness. I am almost completed thirty-nine years and I have not yet adjusted my relation to my fellows on the planet, or to my own work. Always too young or too old, I do not justify myself; how can I satisfy others?

29

THE SNOW-STORM

> Announced by all the trumpets of the sky,
> Arrives the snow, and, driving o'er the fields
> Seems nowhere to alight: the whited air
> Hides hills and woods, the woods, the river,
>   and the heaven
> And veils the farm-house at the garden's end
> The sled and traveller stopped, the courier's feet

Delayed, all friends shut out, the housemates sit,
Around the radiant fireplace, enclosed
In a tumultuous privacy of storm.

Come see the north wind's masonry,
Out of an unseen quarry evermore
Furnished with tile, the fierce artificer
Curves his white bastions with projected roof
Round every windward stake, or tree, or door.
Speeding, the myriad-handed, his wild work
So fanciful, so savage, nought cares he
For number or proportion. Mockingly,
On coop or kennel he hangs Parian wreaths;
A swan-like form invests the hidden thorn:
Fills up the farmer's lane from wall to wall.
Maugre the farmer's sighs; and at the gate
A tapering turret overtops the work
And when his hours are numbered, and the world
Is all his own, retiring, as he were not,
Leaves, when the sun appears, astonished Art
To mimic in slow structures, stone by stone,
Built in an age, the mad wind's night-work,
The frolic architecture of the snow.

30

I do not wish to treat friendships daintily, but with roughest courage. When they are real, they are not glass threads or frostwork, but the solidest thing we know.

31
A visit to Washington, January 31, 1862 where Lincoln reveals a streak of "college boy" humor.

At Washington, January 31, February 1, 2, and 3. Saw Sumner, who, on the 2nd, carried me to Mr. Chase, Mr. Bates, Mr. Stanton, Mr. Welles, Mr. Seward, Lord Lyons and President Lincoln. The President impressed me more favorably than I had hoped. A frank, sincere, well-meaning man, with a lawyer's habit of mind, good clear statement of his fact; correct enough, not vulgar, as described, but with a sort of boyish cheerfulness, or that kind of sincerity and jolly good meaning that our Commencement Days show, in telling our stories over. When he has made his remark, he looks up at you with great satisfaction, and shows all his white teeth, and laughs. . . .

When I was introduced to him, he said, 'Oh, Mr. Emerson, I once heard you say in a lecture, that a Kentuckian seems to say by his air and manners, "Here am I; if you don't like me, the worse for you."'

·FEBRUARY·

1 *A few days after they announced their engagement, Emerson wrote a letter to Lydia Jackson explaining his attitude toward love.*

I delighted myself on Friday with my quite domesticated position & the good understanding that grew all the time, yet I went & came without one vehement word – or one passionate sign. In this was nothing of design. I merely surrendered myself to the hour & to the facts. I find a sort of grandeur in the modulated expressions of a love in which the individual, & what might seem even reasonable personal expectations, are steadily postponed to a regard for truth & the universal love. Do not think me a metaphysical lover. I am a man & hate & suspect the over refiners, & do sympathize with the homeliest pleasures & attractions by which our good foster mother Nature first draws her children together. Yet I am well pleased that between us the most permanent ties should be the first formed & thereon should grow whatever other human nature will.

2 *Two views on friendship by a man who valued the relationship most highly.*

I wish that friendship should have feet, as well as eyes and eloquence. It must plant itself on the ground, before it vaults over the moon. I wish it to be a little of a citizen before it is quite a cherub.

FRIENDSHIP

A ruddy drop of manly blood
The surging sea outweighs.
The world uncertain comes and goes;

The lover rooted stays.
I fancied he was fled, –
And, after many a year,
Glowed unexhausted kindliness,
Like daily sunrise there
My careful heart was free again.
O friend, my bosom said
Through thee alone the sky is arched
Through thee the rose is red
All things through thee take nobler form
And look beyond the earth,
The mill-round of our fate appears
A sun-path in thy worth.
Me too they nobleness has taught
To master my despair;
The fountains of my hidden life
Are through thy friendship fair.

 Emerson the Neoplatonist describes a condition that is common to all meditation and self-reflective thought.

When the act of reflection takes place in the mind, and when we look at ourselves in the light of thought, we discover that our life is embosomed in beauty. Behind us, as we go, all things assume pleasing forms, as clouds do far off ... for it is only the finite that has wrought and suffered; the infinite lies stretched in smiling repose.

 At the Masonic Temple in Boston, Emerson tries to give his audience a clear idea of the meaning of Transcendentalism.

And what is popularly called Transcendentalism among us, is Idealism; Idealism as it appears in 1842. As thinkers, mankind have ever divided into two sects, Materialists and Idealists; the first class founding on experience, the second on consciousness; the first class beginning to think from the data of the senses, the second class perceive that the senses are not final, and say, the senses give us representation of things, but what are the things themselves, they cannot tell. The materialist insists on facts, history, on the force of circumstances, and the animal wants of man; the idealist on the power of Thought and Will, on inspiration, on miracle, on individual culture. These two modes of thinking are both natural but the idealist contends that his way of thinking is in higher nature. He concedes all that the other affirms, admits the impressions of sense, admits their coherency, their use and beauty, and then asks the materialist for his grounds of assurance that things are as his senses represent them. But I, he says, affirm facts not affected by the illusions of sense, facts which are of the same nature as the faculty which reports them, and not liable to doubt; facts which in their first appearance to us assume a native superiority to material facts.

5   *Emerson met the naturalist John Muir during his trip to California in the spring of 1871.*

My dear Muir,

     Here lie your significant Cedar flowers on my table, & in another letter; & I will procrastinate no longer. That singular disease of deferring, which kills all my designs, has left a pair of books brought home to send you months & months ago, still covering their inches on my cabinet, &

the letter & letters which should have accompanied to utter my thanks & lively remembrance, are either unwritten or lost, – so I will send this *peccavi*, as a sign of remorse. I have been far from unthankful, – I have everywhere testified to my friends, who should also be yours, my happiness in finding you, – the right man in the right place, – in your mountain tabernacle, – & have expected when your guardian angel would pronounce that your probation & sequestration in the solitudes & snows had reached their term, & you were to bring your ripe fruits so rare and precious into waiting Society.

6   *Emerson explains why some people are able to express themselves in what he calls "the ecstatic or poetic speech."*

In proportion as a man's life comes into union with the truth, his thoughts approach to a parallelism with the currents of natural laws, so he easily expresses his meaning by natural symbols, or uses the ecstatic or poetic speech. By successive states of mind all the facts of nature are for the first time interpreted. In proportion as his life departs from this simplicity, he uses circumlocution, – by many words hoping to suggest when he cannot say. Vexatious to find poets, who are by excellence the thinking and feeling of the world, deficient in truth of intellect and of affection. Then is conscience unfaithful, and thought unwise.

7   *Emerson never mentions the word reincarnation, but he makes an eloquent case for the divinity and immortality of what we might call "consciousness."*

We cannot describe the natural history of the soul, but we know that it is divine. I cannot tell if these wonderful qualities which house to-day in this mortal frame, shall ever reassemble in equal activity in a similar frame, or whether they have before had a natural history like that of this body you see before you; but this one thing I know, that these qualities did not now begin to exist, cannot be sick with my sickness, nor buried in any grave; but that they circulate through the Universe; before the world was, they were. Nothing can bar them out, nor shut them in, but they penetrate the ocean and land, space and time ... and hold the key to universal nature. I draw from this faith, courage, and hope. All things are known to the soul. It is not to be surprised by any communication. Nothing can be greater than it. Let those fear and fawn who will. The soul is in her native realm, and it is wider than space, older than time, wide as hope, rich as love. Pusillanimity and fear she refuses with a beautiful scorn; they are not for her who putteth on her coronation robes, and goes through universal love to universal power.

8 *The Emersons and the Adamses had been friendly for long time, but this journal entry is more than personal admiration. It reflects Waldo's objective estimate of the man.*

Mr. Adams chose wisely and according to his constitution, when on leaving the Presidency, he went into Congress. He is no literary old gentleman, but a bruiser, and loves the melee. When they talk about his age and venerableness and nearness to the grave, he knows better, he is like one of those old Cardinals, who, as quick as he is chosen Pope, throws away his crutches and his crookedness and is as straight as a boy.

9   *He does not set sail for England until October in this year of 1847, but his imagination calculates both the stormy sea and the luxury of a great ship.*

See this terrible Atlantic stretching its stormy chaos from pole to pole terrible by its storms, by its cold, by its icebergs, by its Gulf stream, the desert in which no caravan loiters, but all hurry as thro' the valley of the Shadow of Death.... Yet see, a man arrives at the margin with 120 dollars in his pocket, and the rude sea grows civil, and is bridged at once for the long three thousand miles to England, with a carpeted floor & a painted & enamelled walls & roof, with books & gay company & feasting & music & wine.

10   *In a note to himself, written in his sixty-seventh year, Emerson simultaneously anticipates what we call "artificial life" and the principles of what has come to be known as "mind-body medicine."*

I do not know that I should feel threatened or insulted if a chemist should take his protoplasm or mix hydrogen, oxygen, and carbon and make an animalcule incontestably swimming and jumping before my eyes. I should only feel that it indicated that the day had arrived when the human race might be trusted with a new degree of power, and its immense responsibility; for these steps are not solitary or local, but only a hint of an advanced frontier supported by an advancing race behind it.

What at first scares the Spiritualist in the experiments of Natural science – as if thought were only finer chyle, fine to aroma – now redounds to the credit of matter, which, it appears, is impregnated with thought and heaven, and is really of God, and not of the Devil, as he had too hastily believed.

11 *Sometimes he could sound chauvinistic about the advantages of being a New Englander.*

The hard soil and four months of snow make the inhabitant of the northern temperate zone wiser and abler than his fellow who enjoys the fixed smile of the tropics.

12 *Contemplating his hero Plato brings him again to his first principle: authenticity.*

But the supreme good is reality; the supreme beauty is reality; and all virtue and felicity depend on the science of the real; for courage is nothing else than knowledge; the fairest fortune that can befall a man is to be guided by his daemon to that which is truly his own.

13 *Ellen Tucker, whom Emerson had married less than two years before, died on February 8th, 1831, at the age of twenty-two.*

Five days are wasted since Ellen went to heaven to see, to know, to worship, to love to intercede.... Reunite us, O thou Father of our spirits.

There is that which passes away and never returns. This miserable apathy, I know, may wear off. I almost fear when it will. Old duties will present themselves with no more repulsive face. I shall go again among my friends with a tranquil countenance. Again I shall be amused, I shall stoop again to little hopes and little fears and forget the graveyard. But will the dead be restored to me? Will the eye that was closed on Tuesday ever beam again in the fulness of love on me? Shall I ever again be able to connect the face of outward nature, the mists of the morn, the star of eve, the flowers, and all poetry, with the heart and life of an enchanting friend? No. There is one birth, and one baptism, and one first love, and the affections cannot keep their youth any more than men.

 GIVE ALL TO LOVE

> Give all to love;
> Obey thy heart;
> Friends, kindred, days,
> Estate, good-fame,
> Plans, credit, and the Muse,
> Nothing refuse.
>
> 'Tis a brave master;
> Let it have scope:
> Follow it utterly,
> Hope beyond hope:
> High and more high
> It dives into noon,
> With wing unspent,
> Untold intent;
> But it is a god,

Knows its own path
And the outlets of the sky.

It was never for the mean;
It requireth courage stout.
Souls above doubt,
Valor unbending,
It will reward.
They shall return
More than they were
And ever ascending.

Leave all for love;
Yet, hear me, yet,
One word more thy heart behoved
One pulse more of firm endeavor,
Keep thee to-day,
Tomorrow, forever,
Free as an Arab
Of thy beloved.

Cling with life to the maid;
But when the surprise,
First vague shadow of surmise
Flits across her bosom young,
Of a joy apart from thee,
Free be she, fancy-free;
Nor thou detain her vesture's hem,
Nor the palest rose she flung
From her summer diadem.

Though thou loved her as thyself,
As a self of purer clay,

Though her parting dims the day,
Stealing grace from all alive,
Heartily know,
When half-gods go,
The gods arrive.

15

Climate is a great impediment to idle persons: we often resolve to give up the care of the weather, but still we regard the clouds and the rain.

16

If Milton, if Burns, if Bryant, is in the world we have more tolerance & more love for the changing sky, the mist, the rain, the bleak overcast day, the indescribable sunrise & the immortal stars. If we believed no poet survived on the planet, nature would be tedious.

17

Emerson finds himself once again delighted with his provocative friend Thoreau.

My good Henry Thoreau made this else solitary afternoon sunny with his simplicity and clear perception. How comic is simplicity in this double-dealing, quacking world. Everything that boy says makes merry with society, though nothing can be graver than his meaning. I told him he should write out the history of his college life, as Carlyle has his tutoring. We agreed that seeing the stars through a telescope would be worth all the astronomical lectures.

18 *These words from a the man who "preached against preaching."*

The true preacher can be known by this, that he deals out to the people his life – life passed through the fire of thought.

19 *Emerson would later take a far more liberal position about women's rights, but in this letter to Wendell Phillips, written in 1853, he is still holding to his principle of believing in the minimum governmental interference.*

My dear sir,

I read the Petition [for women's suffrage] with attention, & with the hope that I should find myself so happy as to do what you bade me. But this is my feeling in regard to the whole matter: I wish that done for their rights which women wish done. If they wish to vote I shall vote that they vote. If they wish to be lawyers & judges, I shall vote that those careers be open to them. But I do not think that wise & wary women wish to be electors or judges; and I will not ask they be made such against their will. If we obtain for them the ballot, I suppose the best women would not vote. By all means let their rights of property be put on the same basis as those of man, or, I should say, on a more favorable ground. And let women go to women, & bring us certain tidings what they want, & it will be imperative on me & on us all to help them get it.

20 *Still only twenty years old, Emerson tries to assess the quality he calls "moral beauty," and pledges himself to the "golden way."*

Material beauty perishes or palls. Intellectual beauty limits admiration to seasons and ages; hath its ebbs and flows of delight.... But moral beauty is lovely, imperishable perfect. It is dear to the child and to the patriarch, to Heaven, Angel, Man.... None that can understand Milton's *Comus* can read it without warming to the holy emotions it panegyrizes.

I would freely give all I ever hoped to be, even when my air-blown hopes were brilliant and glorious, – not as now – to have given down that sweet strain to posterity to do good in a golden way.

21

In probably his most famous and most quoted essay, "Self-Reliance," Emerson exhorts his readers to hear and respect their own intuition.

A man should learn to detect and watch that gleam of light which flashes across his mind from within, more than the lustre of the firmament of bards and sages. Yet he dismisses without notice his thought, because it is his. In every work of genius we recognize our own rejected thoughts; they come back to us with a certain alienated majesty. Great works of art have no more affecting lesson for us than this. They teach us to abide by our spontaneous impression with good-humored flexibility then most when the whole cry of voices is on the other side. Else tomorrow a stranger will say what we have thought and felt all the time, and we shall be forced to take with shame our own opinion from another.

22

Emerson was once caricatured as a "Transparent Eye-Ball" – quite apt in light of this comment.

Truth is the summit of being: justice is the application of it to affairs. . . . A healthy soul stands united with the Just and the True, as the magnet arranges itself with the pole, so that he stands to all beholders like a transparent object betwixt them and the sun, and who so journeys towards the sun, journeys towards that person.

23 *While on his trip to the Southern states in an attempt to improve his health (he was showing signs of the weak lungs that were common in the family), Emerson writes from St. Augustine on February 23, 1827, to his brother Charles.*

Dear Charles,

You are in the heyday of youth when time is marked not by numbering days but by the intervals of mentality the flux & reflux of the soul. One day has a solemn complexion, the next is cheerful, the south wind makes a third poetic, and another is "sicklied o'er with a pale cast of thought," but all are redolent of knowledge & joy. The river of life with you is yet in its mountains and sources bounding & shouting on its way & has not settled down into the monotony of the deep & silent stream. Vouchsafe then to give to your poor patriarchal exhorting brother some of the sweet waters. Write, write. I have heard men say (heaven help their poor wits,) they had rather have ten words *viva voce* from a man than volumes of letters for getting at his opinion. – I had rather converse with them by the interpreter. Politeness ruins conversation.

24 *In his essay, "Education," Emerson bemoans the tendency to haste and the common habit of corporal punishment in dealing with children, and finds in the naturalist a good model for correcting these tendencies.*

Now the correction of this quack practice is to import into Education the wisdom of life. Leave this military hurry and adopt the pace of Nature. Her secret is patience. You know how the naturalist learns all the secrets of the forest, of plants, of birds, of beasts, of reptiles, of fishes, of the rivers in the sea? When he goes into the woods the birds fly before him he finds none; when he goes to the river bank the fish and the reptiles swim away and leave him alone. His secret is patience; he sits down and sits still; he is a statue; he is a log. These creatures have no value for their time, and he must put as low a rate on his.... He sits still; if they approach, he remains passive as the stone he sits upon. They lose their fear. They have curiosity too about him. By and by the curiosity masters the fear, and they come swimming, creeping and flying towards him; and as he is still immovable, they not only resume their own ordinary labors and manners, show themselves to him in their work-day trim, but also volunteer some degree of advances towards fellowship and good understanding with a biped who behaves so civilly and well.

25 *This famous passage from the essay, "History," enunciates a principle closely related to the Hindu scriptures (probably the* Bhagavad Gita) *that Emerson was reading at the time.*

The human mind wrote history, and thus must read it. The Sphinx must solve her own riddle. If the whole of history is in one man, it is all to be explained from individual experience. There is a relation between the hours of our life and the centuries of time. As the air I breathe is drawn from the great repositories of nature, as the light of my book is yielded by a star a hundred millions of miles distant, as the poise of my body depends on the equilibrium of centrifugal and centripetal forces, so the hours should be instructed by the ages and the ages explained by the hours. Of the universal mind each individual man is one more incarnation. All its properties consist in him. Each new fact in his private experience flashes a light on what great bodies of men have done, and the crises of his life refer to national crises.

 Within one of his most famous essays, "The Over-Soul," Emerson makes the case that moments of revelation, the deepest secrets of nature, might be hinted at even when we are engaged in conversation, or in other mundane activities.

In all conversation between two persons tacit reference is made to a third party, to a common nature. That third party or common nature is not social; is impersonal, is God. And so in groups where debate is earnest, and especially on high questions, the company become aware that the thought rises to an equal level in all bosoms, that all have a spiritual property in what was said, as well as the sayer. They all become wiser than they were. It arches over them like a temple, this unity of thought in which every heart beats with nobler sense of power and duty, and thinks and acts with unusual solemnity. All are conscious of attaining to a higher self-possession. It shines for all.

27 *The appeal of Emerson's essay, "Self-Reliance," to young people in the twenty-first century may be found in passages like this one which, by any measure, still appears radical.*

When good is near you, when you have life in yourself, it is not by any known or accustomed way; you shall not discern the foot-prints of any other; you shall not see the face of man; you shall not hear any name; – the way, the thought, the good, shall be wholly strange and new. It shall exclude example and experience.

28 *Emerson's essay on memory covers the whole range of human experience from that of the farmer to Michelangelo, and today still means something to everyone who hears it.*

Remember me means, Do not cease to love me. We remember those things which we love and those things which we hate. The memory of all men is robust on the subject of a debt due to them, or on an insult inflicted on them. . . .

The Persians say, "a real singer will never forget the songs he has once learned." Michael Angelo [*sic*], after having once seen a work of any other artist, would remember it so perfectly that if it pleased him to make use of any portion thereof, he could do so, but in such a manner that none could perceive it.

We remember what we understand, and we understand best what we like; for this doubles our power of attention and makes it our own.

·MARCH·

1

In March many weathers. March always comes if it do not come until May. May generally does not come at all.

2

Emerson knew of the Persian poets as early as 1841, but it was not until three years later that he purchased a copy of Hafiz's Divan, *and working from a German edition he began to translate the Persian poetry he admired so much. In all, he translated over 150 lines, of which the following provides an example.*

I said to heaven that glowed above,
O hide yon sun-filled zone,
Hide all the stars you boast;
For, in the world of love
And estimation true,
The heaped-up harvest of the moon
Is worth one barley-corn at most,
The Pleiads' sheaf but two.

3

Though he would later be gravely disappointed in Daniel Webster's stand on the Slave Act, now, in 1830, he is stirred to profound admiration for the Senator's courage in replying to the chief spokesman of the secessionists.

Read with admiration and delight Mr. Webster's noble speech in answer to Hayne. What consciousness of political rectitude, and what confidence in his intellectual treasure must he have to enable him to take this master's tone.

Mr. Channing said he had great 'self-subsistence.' The beauty and dignity of the spectacle he exhibits should teach men the beauty and dignity of *principles*. This is one that is not blown about by every wind of opinion, but has mind great enough to see the majesty of moral nature and to apply himself in all his length and breadth to it and magnanimously trust thereto.

 On December 21st, 1855, Oliver Wendell Holmes had delivered an oration in New York City which the newspapers reported as being a denunciation of the abolitionists of New England as "traitors to the union." Now, in March, Emerson writes to his friend:

My dear Sir,

I have not seen a true report of your speech, & confess to have drawn my sad thoughts about it from the comments of the journals. I am relieved to know that they misreported you and the more they misreported or the wider you are from their notion of you, the better I divide men as aspirants & desperants. . . . When masses then as cities or churches go for things as they are we take no note of it, we expected as much. . . . But when a scholar, (or disengaged man) seems to throw himself on the dark a cry of grief is heard from the aspirants side exactly proportioned in its intensity to his spiritual rank. . . . The cant of Union like the cant of extending the area of liberty by annexing Texas & Mexico is too transparent for its most impudent repeater to hope to deceive you. And for the Union with Slavery no manly person will suffer a day to go by without discrediting disintegrating and finally exploding it. The "union"

they talk of, is dead & rotten, the real union, that is, the will to keep & renew union, is like the will to keep & renew life, & this alone gives any tension to the dead letter & if when we have broken every several inch of the old wooden hoop will still hold us staunch.

5

Crossing a bare common in snow puddles, at twilight, under a clouded sky, without having in my thoughts any occurrence of special good fortune, I have enjoyed a perfect exhilaration. I am glad to the brink of fear.

6

It seems that we are in debt to Emerson for the concept of the Establishment and its opponents.

There are always two parties, the party of the Past and the party of the Future; the Establishment and the Movement. At times the resistance is reanimated, the schism runs under the world and appears in Literature, Philosophy, Church, State, and social customs. It is not easy to date these eras of activity with any precision, but in this region one made itself remarked, say in 1820 and the twenty years following.

7

The snow still lies even with the tops of the walls across the Walden road, and, this afternoon, I waded through the woods to my grove. A chicadee [*sic*] came out to greet me, flew about within reach of my hands, perched on the nearest bough, flew down into the snow, rested there two seconds, then up again just over my head & busied himself on the dead bark. I whistled to him through my teeth, and (I think, in response) he began at once to whistle. I promised him crumbs, & must not go again to these woods without them. I suppose the best food to carry would be the meat of shagbarks or castille nuts. Thoreau tells me that they are very sociable with wood-choppers, & will take crumbs from their hands.

 This commentary from a man who prided himself on being a good father is a little surprising.

Good manners require a great deal of time, as does a wise treatment of children. Orientals have time, the desert, and stars; the Occidentals have not.

9 *Although he wrote more than 4,500 letters during his lifetime Emerson apparently did not feel really comfortable writing them. This excerpt from a letter to his wife acknowledges the difficulties he had in fully expressing his feelings to her as well as to "every sister & brother of the human race."*

Ah, you always ask me for the that unwritten letter always due, it seems, always unwritten, from year to year, by me to you, dear Lidian—

I fear too more widely true than you mean — always due & unwritten by me to every sister & brother of the human race. I have only to say that I also bemoan myself daily for the same cause — that I cannot write this letter, that I have not stamina & constitution enough to mind the two functions of seraphim & cherub, oh no, let me not use such great words, — rather say that a photometer cannot be a stove . . .

besides am I not, O best Lidian, a most foolish affectionate goodman & papa, with a weak side toward apples & sugar and all domesticities, when I am once in Concord?

10 *Not many writers can be as resilient about criticism as "The George Washington of American Literature."*

I read many friendly & many hostile paragraphs in the journals about my new book, but seldom or never a just criticism. As long as I do not wince, it cannot be that the fault is touched. When the adept applies his galvanic battery now to this part, then to that, on the patient's head, the patient makes no sign, for lungs are sound, & liver, & heart: but, at last, he touches another point, & the patient screams, for it seems there is bronchitis, or is hip disease. And when the critics hit you, I suppose you will know it. I often think I could write a criticism on Emerson that would hit the white.

11 *At the age of twenty-two, Emerson enunciates the basis of what will become one of his most dearly held principles – Compensation.*

All things are double one against the other, said Solomon. The whole of what we know is a system of compensation. Every defect in one manner is made up in another. Every suffering is rewarded; every sacrifice is made up; every debt is paid.

 Emerson appears to agree with modern psychologists, many of whom are concluding that the developmental task of the later years in a person's life is concerned with "spiritual" development.

There is a sublime prudence which is the very highest that we know of man, which, believing in a vast future, – sure of more to come than is yet seen – postpones always the present hour to the whole life; postpones talent to genius, and special results to character. As the merchant gladly takes money from his income to add to his capital, so is a great man very willing to lose particular powers and talents, so that he gain in the elevation of his life. The opening of the spiritual senses disposes men ever to greater sacrifices, to leave their signal talents, their best means and skill of procuring a present success, their power and their fame – to cast all things behind, in the insatiable thirst for divine communications. A purer fame, a greater power rewards the sacrifice. It is the conversion of our harvest into seed.

13

Nothing great was ever achieved without enthusiasm. The way of life is wonderful: it is by abandonment.

14

Skeptic. Pure intellect is the pure devil when you have got off all the masks of Mephistopheles. It is a painful symbol to me that the index or forefinger is always the most soiled of all the fingers.

 Emerson and Caroline Sturgis had met five years before this letter was written. Over the first few years of their connection, they had enough of a flir-

tation that at one point he wrote to her wishing that she could be his "brother," so they might travel together (which appears to have been the most heated point in the romantic relationship). They did correspond at great length and with much feeling. Emerson later introduced her to William Tappan, whom she married in 1847.

Sometimes the air is so full of poetry that the very streets look magnificent, & sometimes we must remember all our walls. The hour is always coming when we shall flow in a full stream without drought, without night, & always to an ocean, that is, to an end commensurate with our force. How pitiful that the circumstance of a city, that is, a thousand houses laid along the ground instead of two or three, should check our thought or feeling, should tend to depress or freeze us. Yet I must bring a stock of health & spirits to town — I shall not find it there. It is always a pleasure to see you and though there were no intercourse it would be a pleasure, for I associate you with all the fine arts and all high truths. But who is fit for friendship? Not one. Who assumes it with mastery & grandeur so that his demeanour speaks for him to all passengers, saying, "I am that finished and holy person who is called a Friend; hinder me not, but cherish my purpose, all men! & all women! For I seek the furtherance of one soul by means that must advance the whole commonwealth of souls."

16 *Emerson here comes as close as he ever does to offering the secret of eternal youth. But of course what he speaks of is not physical youth, but the youthful energy of the spirit.*

Thus there is no sleep, no pause, no preservation, but all things renew, germinate, and spring. Why should we import rags and relics into the new hour? Nature abhors the old, and old age seems the only disease; all others run into this one. We call it by many names, – fever, intemperance, insanity, stupidity, and crime; they are all forms of old age; they are rest, conservatism, appropriation, inertia, not newness, not the way onward. We grizzle every day. I see no need. Whilst we converse with what is above us, we do not grow old, but grow young.

 In the spring of 1849, in preparing what would become volume one of his Collected Works, *Emerson dropped a motto from Plotinus he had been using for some years: "Nature is but an image or imitation of wisdom, the last thing of the soul; nature being a thing which doth only do, but not know." He replaced that motto with some verses of his own, also inspired by Plotinus, and suggesting a dawning of consciousness.*

A subtle chain of countless rings
The next unto the farthest brings;
The eye reads omens where it goes,
And speaks all languages the rose;
And, striving to be man, the worm
Mounts through all the spires of form.

Emerson provides some fascinating insights into the artistic process by once again giving the spirit primacy over fact.

A painter told me that nobody could draw a tree without in some sort becoming a tree; or draw a child by studying the outlines of its form merely – but, by watching for a time his motions and plays, the painter enters into his nature and can then draw him at will in every attitude. . . . I knew a draughtsman employed in a public survey who found that he could not sketch the rocks until their geological structure was first explained to him. In a certain state of thought is the common origin of very diverse works. It is the spirit and not the fact that is identical. By a deeper apprehension, and not primarily by a painful acquisition of many manual skills the artist attains the power of awakening other souls to a given activity.

19 *Although fascinated by science himself, Emerson realized that both the scientific and the spiritual perspective are needed for a significant life.*

Astronomy taught us our insignificance in Nature; showed that our sacred as our profane history had been written in gross ignorance of the laws, which were far grander than we knew; and compelled a certain extension and uplifting of our views of the Deity and his Providence. This correction of our superstitions was confirmed by the new science of geology, and the whole train of discoveries in every department. But we presently saw also that the religious nature in man was not affected by these errors in his understanding. The religious sentiment made nothing of bulk or size, or far or near; triumphed over time as well as space; and every lesson of humility, or justice, or charity, which the old ignorant saints had taught him, was still forever true.

20

In skating over thin ice, our safety is in our speed.

21

Many people believe that given his unflagging optimism, Emerson never acknowledged the imperfections in human nature. This journal entry in 1857 would seem to indicate otherwise.

Men's conscience, I once wrote, is local in spots & veins, here & there, & not in healthy circulation through their system, so that they are unexpectedly good in some passage, & when you infer that they may be depended on in some other case, they heavily disappoint you.... I learn from the photograph & daguerre men, that almost all faces & forms which come to their shops to be copied, are irregular & unsymmetrical, have one eye blue & one grey, the nose is not straight, & one shoulder is higher than the other. The man is physically as well as metaphysically a thing of shreds & patches, borrowed unequally from his good & bad ancestors – a misfit from the start.

22

Emerson's impatience with preachers and what he thought was their hypocritical style remained his lifelong preoccupation.

A man must consider what a rich realm he abdicates when he becomes a conformist. I hear my preacher announce his text & topic as for instance the expediency of the institution of Fast with a coldness that approaches contempt. For do I not know beforehand that not possibly can he say a new or spontaneous word? That with all this affectation of *examining the grounds* of the institution he will do no such thing? Do I not know that he is pledged to himself beforehand not to look at but one side; the permitted side; not as a man, but as a parish minister in Concord? What folly then to say *let us examine,* & purse the mouth with the wrinkles of a judge. He is a retained attorney; and this air of *judgeship* is mere affectation. Even so is it with newspapers; and so with most politicians.

23 *In urging the importance of paying attention to ancient history, Emerson gives his judgment of the ancient Greek people.*

The Greeks are not reflective, but perfect in their senses and in their health, with the finest physical organization in the world. Adults acted with the simplicity and grace of children. They made vases, tragedies and statues, such as healthy senses should – that is in good taste. Such things have continued to be made in all ages, and are now, wherever a healthy physique exists; but, as a class, from their superior organization, they have surpassed all. They combine the energy of manhood with the engaging unconsciousness of childhood.

24 *Once again under the influence of his readings in Hindu poetry and philosophy, Emerson explains the difference between the worldview of the ancient Greeks and that of the Hindus.*

The early Greek philosophers Heraclitus and Xenophanes measure their force on the problem of identity. Diogenes of Appollonia said that unless the atoms were made of one stuff, they could never blend and act with one another. But the Hindus in their sacred writings, express the liveliest feeling, both of the essential identity and of that illusion which they conceive variety to be. "The notions, '*I am*,' and '*This is mine*' which influence mankind, are but the delusions of the mother of the world. Dispel, O Lord of all creatures! the conceit of knowledge which proceeds from ignorance." And the beatitude of man they hold to lie in being freed from fascination.

25

Nothing is secure but life, transition, the energizing spirit. No love can be bound by oath or covenant to secure it against a higher love. No truth so sublime but it may be trivial to-morrow in the light of new thoughts. People wish to be settled; only as far as they are unsettled is there any hope for them.

26

Emerson's wistful observation of his neighbors in 1840 might just as appropriately be heard today — with the figures a little higher, of course.

Ah my poor countrymen! Yankees & Dollars have such inextricable association that the words ought to rhyme. In New York, in Boston, in Providence, you cannot pass two men in the street without the word escaping them in the very moment of encounter, "dollars," "two & a half per cent," "three per cent."

27 *This uncharacteristically morbid journal entry, written when he was twenty-three years old, indicates either that he had a premonition about the dangers of the tuberculosis that was genetic in his family, or else it might be attributed to "sophomore depression," since he had entered the Harvard Divinity School the year before.*

My years are passing away. Infirmities are already stealing on me that may be the deadly enemies that are to dissolve me to dirt, and little is yet done to establish my consideration among my contemporaries, and less to get a memory when I am gone. I confess the foolish ambition to be valued, with qualification. I do not want to be known by them that know me not, but where my name is mentioned I would have it respected. My recollections of early life are not very pleasant.

28 *This is one of Emerson's earliest and most impassioned pleas for the fruitful coexistence of religion and science, and it presents a platform for his redefinition of religion.*

The Religion that is afraid of science dishonours God & commits suicide. It acknowledges that it is not equal to the whole of truth, that it legislates, tyrannizes over a village of God's empire but is not the immutable universal law. Every influx of atheism, of skepticism is thus made useful as a mercury pill assaulting & moving a diseased religion & making way for the truth. . . . Who knows that he has got all the good he might have? We dip our fingers in the sea that would make us invulnerable if we would plunge & swim.

29 *These lines may offer a hint of Emerson's Neo-Platonic notion that ultimately there will be "no blind matter," since all matter is considered to be in an evolutionary state approaching consciousness.*

Then cometh the god, and converts the statues into fiery men, and by a flash of his eye burns up the veil which shrouded all things, and the meaning of the very furniture, of cup and saucer, of chair and clock and tester, is manifest.

30 *Emerson believes himself to have a "tin ear," but is not unaware of the magic and power of music.*

Pythagoras was right who used music as medicine. I lament my want of an ear, but never quite despair of becoming sensible to this discipline. We cannot spare any stimulant or any purgative, we lapse so quickly into flesh & sleep. We must use all the exalters that will bring us into an expansive & productive state, or to the top of our condition. But to hear music, as one would take an ice-cream or a bath, & to forget it the next day, gives me a humble picture.

31 *His essay, "The Poet," is considered by many modern critics to be one of his best. It represents the climax of his long thinking about how he might do for poetry what he had attempted to do for religion in his "Divinity School Address." His ideas are certainly influenced by his familiarity with, and his great admiration for the Persian poets.*

O poet! A new nobility is conferred in groves and pastures, and not in castles or by the sword-blade any longer. The conditions are hard, but equal. Thou shalt leave the world, and know the muse only. Thou shalt not know any longer the times, customs, graces, politics, or opinions of man, but shalt take all from the muse. For the time of towns is tolled from the world by funereal chimes, but in nature the universal hours are counted by succeeding tribes of animals and plants, and by growth of joy on joy. God wills also that thou abdicate a manifold and duplex life, and that thou be content that others speak for thee. Others shall be thy gentlemen and shall represent all courtesy and worldly life for thee; others shall do the great and resounding actions also. . . . The world is full of renunciations and apprenticeships, and this is thine; thou must pass for a fool and a churl for a long season. This is the screen and sheath in which Pan has protected his well-beloved flower, and thou shalt be known only to thine own, and they shall console thee with tenderest love.

·APRIL·

1   *His daughters recalled that he often recited verses aloud while moving around the house, such as this one from his poems about "Nature."*

In Walden woods the chickadee
Runs round the pine and maple tree
Intent on insect slaughter
O tufted entomologist!
Devour as many as you list,
Then drink in Walden water.

2   *Even at the age of sixteen, Emerson demonstrated in his journal (which he was to maintain for sixty years) that he would become a lyrical writer, especially when he dealt with his feelings about the natural world around him. His early work, of course, bears the mark of youthful excess that would later moderate.*

Spring has returned and has begun to unfold her beautiful array, to throw herself on wild-flower couches, to walk around on the hills and summon her songsters to do her sweet homage. The Muses have issued from the library and costly winter dwelling of their votaries, and are gone up to build their bowers on Parnassus, and to melt their ice-bound fountains. The hunter, the shepherd are abroad on the rock and the vallies [*sic*] echo to the merry, merry horn. The Poet, of course, is wandering, while Nature's thousand melodies are warbling to him. This soft bewitching luxury of vernal gates and accompanying beauty overwhelms. It produces a lassitude which is full of mental enjoyment and which we would not exchange for more vigorous pleasure. Although so long as the spell endures, little or nothing is accomplished, nevertheless, I believe it operates to divest the mind of old and worn-out contemplations and bestows new freshness upon life, and leaves behind it imaginations of enchantment for the mind to mould into splendid forms and gorgeous fancies which shall long continue to fascinate, after the physical phenomena which woke them have ceased to delight.

3 *At fifty-eight, Emerson is ready to play the "Sage of Concord," though the air of resignation in his comments is somewhat out of character.*

One capital advantage of old age is the absolute insignificance of a success more or less. I went to town and read a lecture yesterday. Thirty years ago it had really been a matter of importance to me whether it was good and effective. Now it is of none in relation to me. It is long already fixed what I can and what I cannot do.

4 *Emerson did not achieve a particularly distinguished record at Harvard, yet here he sees clearly how wondrous is the progress of an individual's pursuit of knowledge.*

Every cultivated man observes, in his past years, intervals of mentality – and is accustomed to consider the present state of his mind as the result rather of many periods of singular intenseness of thought and feeling than of a perpetual and equable expansion. Corn grows by jumps.

Whoever explores his recollection of those periods, will find that by some causality or some study he has arrived at one of those general ideas that not only epitomize whole trains of thought, but cast a flood of new light upon things inscrutable before; after waiting mostly in the vestibule, had picked up unaware the Master Key, whose wards and springs open every door, and the surprised adventurer goes on astonished from cell to cell, from chamber to chamber, gratified, but overawed at the unexplored extent and opulence of his own possessions.

5 *Emerson was as clear after the Civil War as he had been before on the matter of civil rights.*

You complain that the Negroes are a base class. Who makes and keeps the Jew or the Negro base, who but you, who exclude them from the rights which others enjoy?

6 *On his trip South to restore his health, Emerson meets a man who will become not only one of the more exotic figures in his life but a lifelong and beloved friend: an A T H E I S T !*

A new event is added to the quiet history of my life. I have connected myself by friendship to a man [Achille Murat] who with as ardent a love of truth as that which animates me, with a mind surpassing mine in the variety of its research, and sharpened and strengthened to an energy for action to which I have no pretensions, by advantages of birth and practical connexion with mankind beyond almost all men in the world, – is, yet, that which I had ever supposed only a creature of the imagination – a consistent Atheist, – and a disbeliever in the existence, and, of course, in the immortality of the soul. My faith in these points is strong and I trust, as I live, indestructible. Meantime I love and honour this intrepid doubter. His soul is noble, and his virtue, as the virtue of a Sadducee must always be, is sublime.

7

Where there is no vision, the people perish.

8

Emerson's observation reveals that the ever present preoccupations with financial success and material ostentation are not exclusively modern ones.

We are a puny and fickle folk. Avarice, hesitation, and following are our diseases. The rapid wealth which hundreds in the community acquire in trade, or by the incessant expansion of the population and arts, enchants the eyes of all the rest.

9

The value of reading is succinctly explained to an imaginary skeptic.

'Your reading is irrelevant.' Yes, for you, but not for me. It makes no difference what I read. If it is irrelevant, I read it deeper. I read it until it is pertinent to me and mine, to Nature, and to the hour that now passes. A good scholar will find Aristophanes and Hafiz and Rabelais full of American history.

10

Emerson is wryly amused that his books sell well.

If I should believe the Reviews, and I am always of their

opinion, I have never written anything good. And yet, against all criticism, the books survive until this day.

11 *In this comment we may see why Emerson wanted to be a poet from childhood.*

It was always the theory of literature, that the word of a poet was authoritative and final. He was supposed to be the mouth of the divine wisdom. We rather envied his circumstance than his talent.

12 *He reveals at the age of twenty-three the seeds of doubt about a congregation being superior to an individual when it comes to prayer.*

That it is right to ask God's blessing on us is certainly reasonable. That it is right to enumerate our wants, our sins, even our sentiments, in addresses to this unseen Idea, seems just and natural. And it may probably be averred with safety that there has been no man who has never prayed. That persons whom like circumstances and like feelings assimilate, that a family, that a picked society of friends, should unite in this service, does not, I conceive, violate any precept of just reason. It certainly is a question of more difficult solution whether a promiscuous assemblage, such as is contained in houses of public worship, and collected by such motives, can unite with propriety to advantage in any petition such as is usually offered by one man.

13 *Emerson quietly stumps for living the examined life.*

We are always getting ready to live, but never living. We

have many years of technical education; then many years of earning a livelihood, and we get sick, and take journeys for our health, and compass land and sea for improvement by travelling, but the work of self-improvement, – always under our nose, – nearer than the nearest, is seldom engaged in. A few, few hours in the longest life.

 In 1867 a volume of poems by Emma Lazarus came to Emerson's attention, and a correspondence ensues. The next year Emerson wrote her this letter, which reveals his enthusiasm at being her "tutor." It has very much the tone of Rainer Maria Rilke's famous Letters to a Young Poet, *written thirty-six years later.*

But on poetry there is much to say, that I know not where to begin, & really wish to reply by a treatise of thirty sheets. I should like to be appointed your professor, you being required to attend the whole term. I should be very stern & exigeant, & insist on large readings and writings, & from haughty points of view. For a true lover of poetry must fly wide for his game, & though the sport of poetry is universal & is nearest, yet the successes of poets are scattered in all times & nations, & only in single passages, or single lines, or even words; nay, the best are sometimes in writers of prose. But I did not mean to begin my inaugural discourse on this note; but only sat down to say that I find I am coming to New York at the beginning of next week, & I rely on your giving me an hour, & on your being docile, & concealing all your impatience of your tutor, nay, on your inspiring him by telling him your own results.

15 Emerson, at forty-four, is wistful about the opportunity to reach the larger audience.

Here I am with so much all ready to be revealed to me, as
to other, if only I could be set aglow. I have wished for a
professorship. Much as I hate the church, I have wished the
pulpit that I might have the stimulus of a stated task. . . .

I think I have material enough to serve my countrymen
with thought and music, if only it were not scraps. But men
do not want handfuls of gold-dust, but ingots.

16 In a journal entry reminiscent of his poem, "Two
Rivers," he uses the flowing stream as a metaphor
for what in other places he calls "the big idea."
(Musketaquid is the original name of the Concord
River.)

Thy voice is sweet, Musketaquid; repeats the music of the
rain; but sweeter rivers silent flit through thee, as thou
through Concord plain.

Thou art shut in thy banks; but the stream I love flows
in the water, and flows through rocks and through the air,
and through darkness, and through men, and women. I hear
and see the inundation and eternal spending of the stream,
in winter and in summer, in men and animals, in passion
and thought. Happy are they who hear it.

17 Coming back to health at the end of his Southern
journey in 1827, Emerson is intoxicated with the
sense of his own uniqueness.

Let the glory of the world go where it will, the mind has
its own glory. What it doth, endures. No man can serve

many masters. And often the choice is not given you between greatness in the world and greatness of soul, which you will choose, but both advantages are not compatible. The night is fine; the stars shed down their severe influences upon me, and I feel a joy in my solitude that the merriment of vulgar society can never communicate. There is a pleasure in the thought that the particular tone of my mind at this moment may be new in the universe; that the emotions of this hour may be peculiar and unexampled in the whole eternity of moral being. I lead a new life. I occupy new ground in the world of spirits, untenanted before. I commence a career of thought and action which is expanding before me into a distant and dazzling infinity. Strange thoughts start up like angels in my way and beckon me onward. I doubt not I tread on the highway that leads to Divinity.

18 *On his trip in 1848, Emerson explains why there will be no revolution in England.*

People here expect a revolution. There will be no revolution, none that deserves to be called so. There may be a scramble for money. But as all the people we see want the things we now have, and not better things, it is very certain they will, under whatever change of forms, keep the old system. When I see changed men I shall look for a changed world. Whoever is skillful in heaping money now will be skillful in heaping money again.

19 *The writer's true audience is eloquently defined.*

Happy is he who looks only into his work to know if it will

succeed, never into the times or public opinion; and who writes from the love of imparting certain thoughts and not from the necessity of sale – who writes always to *the unknown friend.*

And the reason why all men honor love, is because it looks up and not down; aspires and not despairs.

Emerson replies to a letter from Colonel Gordon, in which the Northern officer calls the liberated slaves "our faithful friends" and people to be trusted unquestioningly.

I am glad to have this weighty testimony on behalf of the negro. My fear is that he needs every advantage, & at the strongest is not strong enough for his salvation from the cupidity of the white races. Poor Irish, rich planter, and planter's poor tenant, all are alike his enemies. His best hope lies in his proved faculty to make himself useful and indispensable in hot climates: and when the odds of ten to one are taken off, that is to say, when New York & Massachusetts are not made by false law to help Carolina and Georgia to keep him on the ground, I doubt not he will be able to get to his feet & insist on wages for his work.

In the essay, "Representative Men," Emerson sketches profiles of some of his heroes and models. None ranks higher then Plato, and in many ways Emerson's thought can be seen to descend in a direct line from that great philosopher (and the "Neo-

Platonists" who followed him). No surprise, then, that Emerson was sometimes referred to as "The Socrates of Concord."

Philosophy is the account by which the human mind gives to itself of the constitution of the world. Two cardinal facts lie forever at the base; the one, and the two: 1, Unity, or Identity; and 2, Variety. We unite all things by perceiving the law which pervades them; by perceiving the superficial differences and the profound resemblances. But every mental act, – this very perception of identity or oneness, recognizes the difference of things. Oneness and otherness. It is impossible to speak or to think without embracing both.

23 *In 1835 a few Indians, without the consent of their tribe, signed a treaty with the United States government, giving away the Cherokee lands in Georgia for a promised reservation west of the Mississippi. President Martin Van Buren ordered the Army to use force to move the Cherokees off their territory. Emerson attended a protest meeting on April 22 and then wrote a blistering letter, displaying a rare heat and invective that caused him deeply conflicting feelings for years. (Van Buren did not heed either Emerson or other protesters, and hundreds of Cherokee men, women, and children were killed by U. S. soldiers.)*

Sir–

It now appears that the government of the United States choose to hold the Cherokees to this sham treaty . . . and the American President and the Cabinet, the Senate and the House of Representatives neither hear these men [a Cherokee delegation] nor see them, and are contracting to put this active nation into carts and boats and drag them over mountains and rivers into a wilderness a vast distance beyond the Mississippi. . . .

In the name of God, sir, we ask you if this be so . . . does this government think that the people of the United States are become savage and mad? From their mind are the sentiments of love and a good nature wiped clean out? The souls of men, the justice, the mercy that is the heart's heart in all men, from Maine to Georgia does abhor this business.

24 *Emerson always commits himself to the future, to the new, to the evolving.*

A saint, an angel, a chorus of saints, a myriad of Christs, are alike worthless and forgotten by the soul, as the leaves that fall, or the fruit that was gathered in the Garden of Eden in the golden age. A new day, a new harvest, new duties, new men, new fields of thought, new powers call you, and an eye fastened on the past unsuns nature, bereaves me of hope, and ruins me with a squalid indigence which nothing but death can adequately symbolize.

25

Yesterday P. M. I went to the Cliff with Henry Thoreau. Warm, pleasant, misty weather which the great mountain amphitheatre seem to drink in with gladness. A crow's voice filled all the miles of air with sound. A bird's voice, even a piping frog enlivens a solitude & makes world enough for us. At night I went out into the dark & saw a glimmering star & heard a frog & Nature seemed to say Well do not these suffice? Here is a new scene, a new experience. Ponder it, Emerson, & not like the foolish world hanker after thunders & multitudes & vast landscapes, the sea or Niagara.

26 *He echoes his friend Bronson Alcott who wrote that "the true teacher shall have no disciple."*

I have been writing and speaking what were once called novelties, for twenty-five or thirty years, and have not now one disciple. Why? Not that what I said was not true; not that it has not found intelligent receivers; but because it did not go from any wish in me to bring men to me but to themselves. I delight in driving them from me. What could I do if they came to me? – they would interrupt and encumber me. This is my boast that I have no school follower. I should account it a measure of the impurity of insight, if it did not create independence.

27 *Emerson died on Thursday, April 27, 1882, at the age of seventy-nine. On Sunday the 30th he was buried in Concord's Sleepy Hollow Cemetery under a granite stone he had selected, and engraved with the following epitaph, taken from his poem, "The Problem":*

The passive master lent his hand
To the vast soul that o'er him planned.

28

I believe in Omnipresence and find footsteps in grammar rules, in oyster shops, in church liturgies, in mathematics, and in solitudes and galaxies. I am shamed out of my declamations against churches by the wonderful beauty of the English liturgy, an anthology of the piety of ages and nations.

29

Here Emerson engages, as he does on other occasions, in self-condemnation, remorseful at his imagined lack of warmth and passion.

DAYS

Damsels of Time, the hypocritic Days,
Muffled and dumb, like barefoot dervishes,
And marching single in an endless file,
Bring diadems and fagots in their hands.
To each they offer gifts, after his will,—
Bread, kingdoms, stars or sky that holds them all.
I, in my pleached garden, watched the pomp,
Forgot my morning wishes, hastily
Took a few herbs and apples, and the Day
Turned and departed silent. I, too late,
Under her solemn fillet saw the scorn.

30

Emerson, the literary critic, makes a cryptic, if not chauvinistic, remark.

The single word *Madame* in French poetry makes it instantly prose.

· M A Y ·

1   *MAY MORNING*

When the purple flame shoots up,
> And Love ascends his throne,
I cannot hear your songs, O birds,
> For the witchery of my own.

And every human heart
> Still keeps that golden day
And rings the bells of jubilee
> On its own First of May.

2   *THE RHODORA*

On being asked, "Whence is the flower?"

In May, when sea-winds pierced our solitudes,
I found the fresh Rhodora in the woods,
Spreading its leafless blooms in a damp nook,
To please the desert and the sluggish brook,
The purpler petals, fallen in the pool,
Made the black water with their beauty gay;
Here might the red-bird come his plumes to cool,
And court the flower that cheapens his array
Rhodora! If the sages ask thee why
This charm is wasted on the earth and sky,
Tell them, dear, that if eyes were made for seeing.
Then Beauty is its own excuse for being:
Why thou wert here, O rival of the rose!
I never thought to ask, I never knew:
But in my simple ignorance, suppose

The self-same Power that brought me there
brought you.

3 *Emerson anticipates one of the principles of holism*
— the whole is greater than the sum of its parts —
and at the same time prefigures the basis of general
semantics: object 1 is not object 2 is not object 3, etc.

We have no theory of animated Nature. When we have, it
will be the true Classification. Perhaps the study of the cat-
tle on the mountainside as they graze, is more suggestive
of truth than the inspection of their parts in the dissection-
room. . . .

I wrote once before that the true philosophy of man
should give a theory of Beasts & Dreams. A German dis-
patched them both by saying that Beasts are dreams, or
"the nocturnal side of Nature."

4 *One poet takes the measure of another.*

I saw Tennyson first at the house of Coventry Patmore,
where we dined together. . . . I was contented with him at
once. He is tall, scholastic-looking, no dandy — but a great
deal of plain strength about him, &, though cultivated,
quite unaffected. Quiet sluggish sense & strength, refined,
as all English are — and good humoured. The print of his
head in Horne's book is too rounded & handsome. There is
in him an air of general superiority, that is very satisfac-
tory. . . . I told Tennyson, that I had heard from his friends
very good accounts of him & I and they were persuaded
that it was important to his health, an instant visit to Paris;

and that I was to go on Monday if he was ready. He was very good humoured and affected to think that I should never come back alive from France, it was death to go.

5   *This journal entry, written just twelve days before his nineteenth birthday, demonstrates how early Emerson became self-critical and began taking sharp analytical stock of himself.*

Has any other educated person lived so many years and lost so many days? I do not say acquired so little for by any ease of thought and certain looseness of mind I have perhaps been the subject of as many ideas as many of mine age. But mine approaching maturity is attended with a goading sense of emptiness & wasted capacity; with the conviction that vanity has been content to admire the little circle of natural accomplishments, and has traveled again & again the narrow round, instead of adding sedulously the gems of knowledge to their number. Too tired too indolent to travel up the mountain path which leads to good learning, to wisdom & to fame, I must be satisfied with beholding with an envious eye the laborious journey & final success of my fellows, remaining stationary myself until my inferiors & juniors have reached & outgone me.

6   *At the climax of his eulogy for his good friend, Henry David Thoreau, who died at only forty-seven years of age, Emerson correctly predicts that Thoreau's influence will be everlasting.*

There is the flower known to botanists, one of the same genus with our summer plant called "Life-Everlasting," a

Gnaphalium like that, which grows on the most inaccessible cliffs of the Tyrolese mountains, where the chamois dare hardly venture, and which the hunter, tempted by its beauty and by his love (for it is immensely valued by the Swiss maidens), climbs the cliffs to gather, and is sometimes found dead at the foot, with the flower in his hand. It is called by botanists the *Gnaphalium leontopodium* but by the Swiss, *Edelweisses*, which signifies *Noble Purity*. Thoreau seemed to me to be living in the hope of gathering this plant, which belonged to him of right. The scale on which his studies proceeded was so large as to require longevity, and we were the less prepared for his sudden disappearance. The country knows not yet, or in the least part, how great a son it has lost. It seems an injury that he should leave in the midst of his broken task which none else can finish, a kind of indignity to so noble a soul that he should depart out of Nature before yet he has been really shown to his peers for what he is. But he, at least, is content. His soul was made for the noblest society; he had in a short life exhausted the capabilities of this world; wherever there is knowledge, wherever there is virtue, wherever there is beauty, he will find a home.

7   *Though his cool demeanor may have suggested that he was not a passionate man, Emerson's enthusiasm to find his "place to stand" clearly shows otherwise.*

Passion, though a bad regulator, is a powerful spring. . . . 'Tis the heat which sets our human atoms spinning, overcomes the friction of crossing thresholds and first addresses in society, and gives us a good start and speed, easy to continue when once it is begun.

8

There are days which occur in this climate, at almost any season of the year, wherein the world reaches its perfection, when the air, the heavenly bodies, and the earth make a harmony, as if Nature would indulge its offspring.

9

Even his complaints are mixed with poetic prose, especially when he writes to his wife Lidian.

I hope our town whose name I duly superscribe to my epistles will not come to read Discord through Lidian's lenses gray. The innocent river flows through the flats under my eye yet unknowing that his friend's friend loves the surly sea's roar better than his childish murmuring. Ah he would look me pathetically in the face, did he imagine, that I his almost sole votary, (for I fear that he hath not on his banks another watcher of his poetical aspects) meditated a desertion of his gentle side. I have promised him a song too, whenever the tardy callow muse shall new moult her feathers. River large & ink stand little, deep & deep would blend their voices.... Lidian what have you done with my Plymouth sermon. I forgot twice to take it away. All that is important is to keep it out of sight.... I cannot stay next Friday O magnetic mine, for, Saturday night I am to lecture at Waltham & Sunday preach there on an old agreement, which abridges my brief week. One thing more among the facts, – please never write my name with the prefix Rev. Have I not told you, dear Lidian, that I meet much more reverence than I know what to do with?

10   *On the same day that Emerson passes on a tip reminding us that "the shoemaker should stick to his last," he flirts with vegetarianism — but ultimately does not "convert."*

If you have no talent for scolding, do not scold; if none for explaining, do not explain; if none for giving parties, do not give parties, however graceful or needful these acts may appear in others.

I begin to dislike animal food. I had whimsies yesterday after dinner which disgusted me somewhat. The man will not be much better than the beast he eats.

11   *Despite his feelings that its churches are "bare & poor" compared to those of Rome and Naples, Emerson is positively rhapsodic about Florence where the atmosphere for artists earns his full approval.*

And how do you like Florence? Why, well. It is pleasant to see how affectionately all the artists who have resided here a little will speak of getting home to Florence. And I found at once that we live here with much more comfort than in Rome or Naples. Good streets, industrious population, spacious well furnished lodgings, elegant & cheap Caffès, the splendid galleries and no beggars. . . . I took a hasty glance at the gates of the Baptistry which [Michael] Angelo said ought to be the gates of paradise ("*degne chiudere il Paradiso*"), and then of his own David & hasted to the Tribune & to the Pitti Palace. I saw the statue that enchants the world. And truly the Venus deserves to be visited from far. Not adequately represented by the plaster casts as the Apollo & the Laocoon are. I must go again and see this statue. Then I went round this cabinet & gallery & galleries till I was well nigh "dazzled & drunk with beauty." I think no man has an idea of the powers of painting until he has come hither. Why should painters study at Rome? Here, here. . . .

12   *Emerson reaches for a definition of a writer's verac-ity, one of his favorite speculations.*

All writings must be in a degree exoteric, written to a human *should* or *would,* instead of to the fatal *is*: this holds even of the bravest and sincerest writers. Every writer is a skater, and must go partly where he would and partly where the skates carry him; or a sailor who can only land where sails can be blown. And yet it is to be added, that high poetry exceeds the fact, or nature itself, just as skates allow the good skater far more grace than his best walk-ing would show, or sails more than riding. The poet writes from a real experience, the amateur feigns one. Of course, one draws the bow with his fingers, and the other with the strength of his body; one speaks with his lips, and the other with a chest voice. Talent amuses, but if your verse has not a necessary and autobiographic basis, though under what-ever gay poetic veils, it shall not waste my time.

13   *Here Emerson uses the the East as a metaphor for the sunrise and newness, but it may also may be a half-conscious reference to the influence of Eastern thought on his writing.*

What a benefit if a rule could be given whereby the mind could at any moment *east* itself, & find the sun. . . .
But the truest state of mind, rested in, becomes false.

Thought is the manna which cannot be stored. It will be sour if kept, & tomorrow must be gathered anew. Perpetually must we East ourselves, or we get into irrecoverable error, starting from the plainest truth & keeping as we think the straightest road of logic. It is by magnifying God, that men become Pantheists; it is by piously personifying him, that they become idolaters.

 More than ten years after writing the previous entry, Emerson, in his essay "Illusions," amplifies his understanding of the basis of Hindu theology.

In the history of intellect no more important fact than the Hindoo theology, teaching that the beatitudes or Supreme Good is to be obtained through science; namely, by perception of the real and unreal, setting aside matter, and qualities and affections, or emotions and persons and actions as *Maias* or illusions, and thus arriving at the contemplation of the One Eternal Life and Cause and a perpetual approach and assimilation to Him; thus as escaping new births and transmigration.

The highest object of their religion was to restore that bond by which their own self (*atman*) was linked to the eternal Self (*paramatman*); to recover that unity which had been clouded and obscured by the magical illusions of reality; by the so-called Maia of Creation.

15 *Emerson writes his friend Thomas Carlyle with news of a new "toy" — a piece of land on which he anticipates building a two-story house that looks out at the New Hampshire mountains. The woodlot, of course, will later become the site of a far*

more modest structure built and lived in by Henry David Thoreau.

I too have a new plaything, the best I ever had – a wood-lot. Last fall I bought a piece of more than 40 acres, on the border of a little lake a half a mile wide and more, called Walden Pond – a place to which my feet have for years been accustomed to bring me once or twice a week at all seasons. . . . Some of the wood is an old growth, but most of it has been cut off within twenty years and is growing thriftily. In these May days, when maples, poplars, oaks, birches are in their spring glory, I go thither every afternoon, and cut with my hatchet an Indian path through the thicket all along the bold shore, and open the finest pictures. . . .

At a good distance in from the shore the land rises to a rocky head, perhaps sixty feet above the water. . . . There I hope to go with book and pen when good hours come.

16 *Like his friend Thoreau, Emerson takes a stand against philanthropy – but he does remind us, in his essay on "Domestic Life," that we owe each other the gift of humanity.*

To give money to a sufferer is only a come-off. It is only a postponement of the real payment, a bribe paid for silence – a credit system in which a paper promise to pay answers for the time, instead of liquidation. We owe to man higher succors then food and fire. We owe man man. If he is sick, is unable, is mean-spirited and odious, it is because there is so much of his nature which is unlawfully withholden from him. He should be visited in this his prison with rebuke to the evil demons, with manly encouragement, with no mean-spirited offer of condolences because you have not money, or mean offer of money as the utmost benefit, but by your heroism, by your purity by your faith. You are to bring with you that spirit which is understanding – health and self-help. To offer him money in lieu of these, is to do him the same wrong as when the bridegroom offers his betrothed virgin a sum of money to release him from his engagement. The great depend on their heart, not their purse.

17 *Mount Monadnock in southern New Hampshire was among Emerson's favorites. It was the mountain he hoped to view from the house he had envisioned for his land at Walden Pond. In a very long poem, Emerson uses the mountain as a metaphor for a purposeful Creation, and the following lines, at the poem's climax, give some flavor of the romantic speculations he explores throughout the work.*

MONADNOC

To myriad kinds and times one sense,
The constant mountain doth dispense;
Shedding on all its snows and leaves
One joy it joys, one grief it grieves.
Thou seest, O watchman tall,
Our towns and races grow and fall.
And imagest the stable goods
For which we all our lifetime grope,
In shifting form the formless mind,
And thought the substance us elude,
We in thee shadow find.

Thou, in our astronomy
An opaker [*sic*] star,
See haply from afar,
Above the horizon's hoop
A moment, by the railway troop
As o'er some bolder height they speed
By circumspect ambition
By errant gain
By feasters and the frivolous, –
Recallest us,
And makest sane.

Mute orator! well skilled to plead,
And send conviction without phrase,
Thou dost succor and remede
The shortness of our days,
And promise, on thy Founder's truth,
Long morrow to this mortal youth.

 Emerson regrets that, despite all the world's religions and philosophies, no verifiable explanation of the origin and future of the cosmos exists.

We have more traditions than the most resolute skeptic has yet interrogated or even guessed. How few cosmogonies have we. A few have a kind of classical character & we let them stand, for a world-builder is a rare man. And yet what ghosts & hollow formless dream-gear these theories are; how crass and inapplicable! how little they explain; what a poor handful of facts in this plentiful Universe they touch; Let me see. – Moses, Hesiod, Egyptian lore of Isis

& Osiris, Zoroaster, — With these few rude poems or extracts from rude poems the nations have been content when any clever boy black or white has anywhere interrupted the stupid uproar or by a sharp question – "Would anyone please tell me whence I came hither?"

19 *Though he has said that "'tis a problem of metaphysics to define the province of Fancy and Imagination," Emerson nevertheless makes it eminently clear how he perceives them to be different.*

Imagination is central; fancy, superficial. Fancy relates to surface, in which a great part of life lies. The lover is rightly said to fancy the hair, eyes, complexion of the mate. Fancy is a wilful, imagination a spontaneous act; fancy [is] a play as with dolls and puppets which we choose to call men and women; imagination, a perception and affirming of a real relation between a thought and some material fact. Fancy amuses; imagination expands and exalts us. Imagination uses an organic classification. Fancy joins by accidental resemblance, surprises and amuses the idle, but is silent in the presence of great passion and action. Fancy aggregates; imagination animates. Fancy is related to color; imagination, to form. Fancy paints; imagination sculptures.

20

Conversation . . . is the right metaphysical professor. This is the true school of philosophy – this the college where you learn what thoughts are, what powers lurk in those fugitive gleams, and what becomes of them; how they make history.

21 *Emerson records on May 21st that he had spent the previous day with Thoreau and gives us a clear picture of what a fastidious and perceptive naturalist his friend really was.*

He was in search of yellow violet (*pubescens*) and *menyanthes* which he waded into the water for & which he concluded, on examination, had been out five days. Having found his flowers, he drew out of his breast pocket his diary & read the names of all the plants that should bloom on this day, 20 May; whereof he keeps account as a banker when his notes fall due. . . . He heard a note which he calls that of the nightwarbler, a bird he has never identified, has been in search of for over twelve years; which, always, when he sees it, is in the act of diving down into a tree or bush, & which 'tis vain to seek; the only bird that sings indifferently by night & by day. I told him, he must beware of finding & booking him, lest life should have nothing more to show him. He said, "What you seek in vain for half your life, one day you come full upon all the family at dinner. You seek him like a dream, and as soon as you find him, you become his prey." He thinks he could tell by the flowers what day of the month it is, within two days.

22 *The "club of clubs" that Emerson refers to in this letter to his dear friend, Margaret Fuller, is a group that in July 1840 will publish the first issue of the magazine, "The Dial," to which Emerson will contribute much support and a good deal of writing.*

My dear,
    Next Wednesday the club of clubs meet at my house.

Will you not come & see me & inspire our reptile wits. Mr. Ripley said he should like to bring you. I've asked Mrs. S. Ripley & Sarah Clarke. Henry Hedge, Theodore Parker, Alcott, & Henry Thoreau will certainly be here. So that you see if the main senate should not be prosperous, we can sit in committees & settle all our affairs.... One great thing I have to say, this, namely that you will not like Alcott's papers; that I do not like them; that Mr. Ripley will not; & yet I think, on the whole, they ought to be printed pretty much as they stand, with his name in full. They will be differently read with his name or without. Give them his name and those who know him will have his voice in their ear whilst they read, & the sayings will have a majestical sound. Some things are very good: for the most part, they are open to the same fault as his former papers, of being cold vague generalities. Yet if people are properly acquainted with the prophet himself, – & his name is getting fast into the stellar regions, – these will have a certain fitting Zoroastrian style.

23

> The south-wind brings
>   Life, sunshine and desire
> And on every mount and meadow
>   Breathes aromatic fire.

Emerson's brother Robert (Bulkeley), who was four years his junior, was mentally impaired and for most of his fifty-two years was either institutionalized or "boarded out." When he finally died,

Waldo wrote his older brother William to give him the news.

Dear William,

Mrs Reuben Hoar has just come from Littleton to tell me that Bulkeley died this morning at 7 o'clock. . . . He had, about the end of February, a sort of fit which Dr. Bartlett thought apoplectic, though of short duration, and after that was feeble & lost flesh . . . he had not got out of doors again, & resumed work a little & yesterday was abroad, feeling comfortable. This morning he did not come down at his usual hour, and Mrs Hoar went to him, and asked him if he would not come down to breakfast. He appeared surprised to know that it was past the hour, but would not come down; when she went up again, he was speechless, & soon dead. . . . It seems, he said this morning, to Mr Hoar, that he thanked him & Mrs H for their kindness to him. . . . It is very sorrowful, but the sorrow is in the life & not in the death. In the last few years he has never seemed to enjoy life, and I am very happy to hear of this singular piece of sanity, this premonition of approaching death, which led to the thanking Mr. Hoar.

25 *Once again Emerson wrestles with formulating the concept of "the one in the many, the many in the one," the Hindu principle enunciated in the Bhagavad Gita, which he was reading – and rereading.*

Who shall define to me an Individual? I behold with awe & delight many illustrations of the One Universal mind. I see my being imbedded in it. As a plant in the earth so I grow in God. I am only a form of him. He is the soul of

Me. I can even with a mountainous aspiring say, I am God, by transferring me out of the flimsy & unclean precincts of my body, my fortunes, my private will; & meekly retiring upon the holy austerities of the Just & the Loving – upon the secret fountains of Nature. That thin & difficult ether, I can also breathe. The mortal lungs & nostrils burst & shrivel, but the soul itself needeth no organs – it is all element & all organ. Yet why not always so? How came the Individual thus armed and impassioned to parricide, thus murderously inclined ever to traverse & kill the divine life? Ah wicked Manichee! Into that dim problem I cannot enter. A believer in unity, a seer of Unity, I yet behold two.

26 *Emerson could sound as bellicose as the Union generals when considering the appropriate fate of the "Rebels." He had, after all, been raised in the shadow of the American Revolution, and through his family's history, was no stranger to war.*

'Tis far better that the rebels have been pounded instead of negociated [*sic*] into a peace. They must remember it, and their inveterate brag will be humbled, if not cured. George Minot used to tell me over the wall, when I urged him to go to town meetings and vote that "votes did no good; what was done so wouldn't last, but what was done by bullets would stay put." General Grant's terms certainly look a little too easy.

27 *One of Emerson's biographers, Gay Wilson Allen, says that after reading Mme. De Staël's Germany he had been impressed with her statement that*

"Almost all the axioms of physics correspond with the axioms of morals." Allen believed that statement led Emerson to conclude the following.

The universe is pervaded with myriads of secret analogies that tie together its remotest parts as the atmosphere of a summer morn[in]g is filled with innumerable gossamer threads running in every direction but revealed by the beams of the rising sun. So when the soul which in its activity is light begins to throw out its rays, it finds it has been living amidst beauty all unperceived, amidst power with which it has never armed itself, and wisdom, yet was a fool.

28 *In another section of his eulogy to his friend Thoreau, Emerson expresses his wistfulness that his friend was content to remain so secluded and not take up one of the world's "great" challenges.*

Had his genius been only contemplative, he had been fitted to his life, but with his energy and practical ability he seemed born for great enterprise and for command; and I so much regret the loss of his rare powers of action, that I cannot help counting it a fault in him that he had no ambition. Wanting this, instead of engineering for all America, he was the captain of a huckleberry-party. Pounding beans is good to the end of pounding empires one of these days; but if, at the end of years, it is still only beans!

29

The epochs of our life are not in the visible facts of our choice of a calling, our marriage, our acquisition of an office, and the like, but in a silent thought by the way-side as we walk; in a thought which revises our entire manner of life, and says, "Thus hast those done, but it were better thus."

30

Emerson defines true authenticity in the individual as being a function not of the ego and its worldly preoccupations, but of the soul and its relationship to the spiritual.

The intuition of the moral sentiment is an insight of the perfection of the laws of the soul. These laws execute themselves. They are out of time, out of space, and not subject to circumstance. Thus in the soul of man there is a justice whose retributions are instant and entire. He who does a good deed is instantly ennobled. He who does a mean deed is by the action itself contracted. He who puts off impurity, thereby puts on purity. If a man is at heart just, then so far is he God; the safety of God, the immortality of God, the majesty of God do enter into that man with justice. If a man dissemble, deceive, he deceives himself, and goes out of acquaintance with his own being. A man in the view of absolute goodness, adores, with total humility. Every step so downward, is a step upward. The man who renounces himself, comes to himself.

31

In passages like this we can see why Emerson has achieved a fame even greater than Benjamin Franklin for the grace of his epigrammatic advice.

The young man relying on his instincts who has only a good intention is apt to feel ashamed of his inaction & the slightness of his virtue when in the presence of the active & the zealous leaders of the philanthropic enterprizes [*sic*] of Universal Temperance, Peace, & Abolition of Slavery. He only loves like Cordelia after his duty.

· J U N E ·

1

The green grass is bowing,
    The morning wind is in it,
'Tis a tune worth thy knowing,
    Though it change every minute.

2

For Emerson, every child is a gifted child, and his recommendation for teaching them sounds like the charter of a "progressive" school.

Can you not baffle the impatience of the child by your tranquility?

Can you not wait for him as Nature and Providence do? Can you not keep for his mind and ways, for his secret, the same curiosity you give to the squirrel, snake, rabbit, and the sheldrake and the deer. He has a secret; wonderful methods in him; he is – every child – a new style of man; give him time and opportunity. Talk of Columbus and Newton! I tell you the child just born in yonder hovel is the beginning of a revolution as great as theirs. But you must have the believing and prophetic eye. Have the self-command you wish to inspire. Your teaching and your discipline must have the reserve and taciturnity of Nature. Teach them to hold their tongues by holding your own.

Say little; do not snarl; do not chide; but govern by the eye. See what they need, and the right thing is done.

3

In a journal entry as cryptic as a zen koan Emerson seems both awestruck and wistful about two subjects he has usually treated with great seriousness.

Friendship, like the immortality of the soul,
is too good to be believed.

 *Emerson had always believed that his brother
Charles was the most gifted member of the family.
His sudden death in 1836 affected Waldo so much
that he had difficulty dealing with it, and as he
often did in such extreme circumstances, he turned
to his aunt, Mary Moody Emerson, whom he considered his "dearest friend."*

And that is the end, on this side of heaven, of his extraordinary promise – the union of such shining gifts – grace
and genius and sense and virtue.... In him I have lost all
my society. I sought no other and formed my habits to live
with him. I deferred to him on so many questions and trusted him more than myself that I feel as if I had lost the best
part of myself. In him were the foundations of so solid a
confidence and friendship that all the years to come of life
leaned upon him. His genius too was a fountain inexhaust-
ible of thoughts and kept me ever curious and expectant.
Nothing was too great, nothing too beautiful for his grasp
or his expression and as brilliant as his power of illustra-
tion was he stuck like a mathematician to his truth and
never added a syllable for display ... he has never stopped
growing but has ripened from month to month. Indeed the
weight of his thoughts and the fresh and various forms in
which he instantly clothed them has made Shakespear [*sic*]
more conceivable to me, as also Shakespear was almost the
only genius whom he wholly loved.

5

There are persons both of superior character & intellect whose superiority quite disappears when they are put together. They neutralize, anticipate, puzzle and belittle each other.

 Moncure Conway was a graduate of the Harvard Divinity School and is considered one of the second-generation Transcendentalists who had been influenced by Emerson. In 1860 he began a magazine called the "Dial," named in honor of the original Boston journal with which Emerson was associated. He had arranged for Emerson to write an article for him, but in this letter we see that even a great man of letters can find it difficult to fulfill his writing promises.

My dear Sir,

When I shrink sometimes on the thought of your expectations & my abysmal non-performance, I try to assure myself that I never dared to make any exact promises, but only good intentions, to crystallize into act at a long day. Still whenever prudence or diffidence I may have used, I confess, my dulness & incapacity at work has far exceeded any experience or any fear I had of it. It has cost me more time lately to do nothing, in many attempts to arrange & finish old MSS for printing, then ever I think before to do what I could best. For the scrap of paper that I was to send you, after Philadelphia, – Dr. Furness, when he came here, told me, I was not to go. Then I kept it to put into what will not admit anything peaceably, my "Religion" chapter, which has a very tender stomach, on which nothing will lie. They say, the ostrich hatches her egg by standing off & looking at it, and that is my present secret of authorship.

7 *No one has ever defined the obligation of the intellectual in society more clearly than Emerson, who himself was the incarnate example of "Man Thinking."*

The tradesman scarcely ever gives an ideal worth to his work, but is ridden by the routine of his craft, and the soul is subject to dollars. The priest becomes a form; the attorney a statute-book; the mechanic a machine; the sailor a rope of the ship.

In this distribution of functions the scholar is the delegated intellect. In the right state he is *Man Thinking.* In the degenerate state, when the victim of society, he tends to become a mere thinker, or still worse, the parrot of other men's thinking.

In this view of him, as Man Thinking, the theory of his office is contained. Him Nature solicits with all her placid, all her monitory pictures; him the past instructs; him the future invites. Is not indeed every man a student, and do not all things exist for the students behoof? And, finally, is not the true scholar the only true master?

8 *In the summer of 1827 Emerson spent much of his time roaming the hills and fields of the Concord he had known since childhood. In his journals he mused on permanence and impermanence in nature.*

These are the same, but I am not the same,
But wiser than I was, and wise enough,
Not to regret the changes, tho they cost
Me many a sigh. Oh, call not nature dumb;
These trees and stones are audible to me,
These idle flowers, that tremble in the wind,
I understand their faery syllables,
And all their sad significance.

9 *Charles Sumner, a senator from Massachusetts, was
a good friend of Emerson's. Both of them would
become important figures in the antislavery movement, but in this letter Emerson is content to express
his general admiration for Sumner's work as a
senator.*

My dear Sumner,

I thank you heartily for your brave temperate & sound
Speeches, – all rooted in principles, and, what is less to my
purpose, but grateful also to me, – rooted in history. It is
an immense advantage to an honest man, – which seems
none, at the moment, – that all the argument & the elevation of tone should be on his side. For I hold it certain that
water & intelligence *work down,* & that each man takes
counsel of him whom he feels to be a little higher than he;
and this one of the next higher; & so on, & up, in an
ascending gradation; so that, however slowly, the best
opinion is always becoming known as such. I can easily
believe you have had a rude winter of it, on your "north
wall of opposition"; – but not comfortless, – when you see
the vast importance which the times and circumstance

have added to the good fortune of Massachusetts in having you in the Senate in these eventful years. Well done!
But no release yet to be so much as thought of! Stand fast
to the end! making all of us your honorers & debtors; and
none more than Yours faithfully,

10 *Once again Emerson sees the thorny problems of
preparing for publication or the lecture platform,
and clearly discerns the conflict between principle
and the marketplace.*

'Tis very costly, this thinking for the market in books or
lectures: as soon as anyone turns the conversation on my
"Representative men," for instance, I am instantly sensible
that there is nothing there for conversation, that the argument is all pinched & illiberal & popular.

Only what is private, & yours, & essential, should ever
be printed or spoken. I will buy the suppressed part of the
author's mind; you are welcome to all he published.

11

He who knows the most, he who knows what sweets and
virtues are in the ground, the water, the plants, the heav-
ens, and how to come at these enchantments, is the rich
and royal man.

12 *Emerson applies his own rules of Undulation and
Compensation (or what might be called his version
of the Taoist yin-yang dynamic) to the environ-
ments of solitude and society.*

Solitude is naught & society is gone. Alternate them & the good of each is seen. You can soon learn all that society can teach you for one while. A foolish routine, an indefinite multiplication of balls, concerts, rides, theatres, can teach you no more than a few can. Then retire & hide; & from the valley behold the mountain. Have solitary prayer & praise. Love the garden, the barn, the pasture, & the rock. There digest & correct the past experience, blend it with the new & divine life, & grow with God. After some interval when these delights have been sucked dry, accept again the opportunities of society. The same scenes revisited shall wear a new face, shall yield a higher culture. And so on. Undulation, Alternation, is the condition of progress, all of life.

13   *Emerson reminds us that the road to enlightenment is not necessarily through Herculean labors, but in the mundane problems right in front of us.*

We fancy we have fallen into bad company and squalid condition, low debts, shoe bills, broken glass to pay for, pots to buy, butcher's meat, sugar, milk, and coal. "Set me some great task, ye gods! and I will show my spirit." "Not so," says the good Heaven; "plod and plough, vamp your old coats and hats, weave a shoestring; great affairs and the best wine by and by." Well, 'tis all phantasm; and if we weave a yard of tape in all humility and as well as we can, long hereafter we shall see it was no cotton tape at all but some galaxy which we braided, and that the threads were Time and Nature.

14   *Even in the activities of preaching and worshiping Emerson makes the case for each of us doing it in*

our own way. There are echoes here of William Blake's statement, "Thou art a man, God is no more, thine own humanity learn to adore."

Let me admonish you, first of all, to go alone; to refuse the good models even those which are sacred in the imagination of men, and dare to love God without mediator or veil. Friends enough you shall find who will hold up to your emulation Wesleys and Oberlins, Saints and Prophets. Thank God for these good men, but say "I also am a man." Imitation cannot go above its model. The imitator dooms himself to hopeless mediocrity. The inventor did it because it was natural to him, and so in him it has a charm. In the imitator something else is natural, and he bereaves himself of his own beauty, to come short of another man's.

15 *Emerson rails against the widespread, religion-dominated conformity of his time (1838).*

The Unbelief of the age is attested by the loud condemnation of trifles. Look at our silly religious papers. Let a minister wear a cane or a white hat, go to a theatre, or avoid a Sunday school, let a school book with a Calvinistic sentence or a Sunday school book without one, be heard of, & instantly all the old grannies squeak & gibber & do what they call sounding an alarm, from Bangor to Mobile. Alike nice & squeamish is its ear; you must on no account say "stink;" or "damn."

16

It will hereafter be noted that the events of culture in the

Nineteenth Century were, the new importance of the genius of Dante, Michael Angelo [*sic*], and Raffaele [*sic*] to Americans; the reading of Shakespeare; and, above, all the reading of Goethe. Goethe was the cow from which all their milk was drawn.

They all took the "European complaint" and went to Italy. Then there was an uprise of Natural History, and in London, if you would see the fashionable and literary celebrities, you must go to the *soirées* of the Marquis of Northampton, President of the Royal Society, or to the Geological Club at Somerset House.

It seems, however, as if all the young gentlemen and gentlewomen of America spent several years in lying on the grass and "watching the grand movements of the clouds in the summer sky" during this century.

17 *Proof that even a genius can feel the heat, and that the weather can paralyze creativity.*

A cool damp day, a cool evening, the first interruption we have we have had to the energy of the heat of the last 8 or 10 days wherein the mercury has ranged from 70 to 90. When the cool wind blows, the serene muse parts her fragrant locks, & looks forth.

What canst thou say, high daughter of God! to the waiting son of man? What canst thou teach to elevate these low relations, or to interpret them; to fill the day; to dispel the languor & dulness; & bring heaven into the housedoor? Ah! say it, & to me.

18 *In one of his most famous essays, "Self-Reliance," Emerson utters words that will be associated with*

him forever, as he urges his reader to strive always for authenticity.

A foolish consistency is the hobgoblin of little minds, adored by little statesmen and philosophers and divines. With consistency a great soul has simply nothing to do. He may as well concern himself with his shadow on the wall. Speak what you think now in hard words and to-morrow speak what to-morrow thinks in hard words again, though it contradict everything you said today, – 'Ah, so you shall be sure to be misunderstood.' – Is it so bad then to be misunderstood? Pythagoras was misunderstood, and Socrates, and Jesus, and Luther, and Copernicus, and Galileo and Newton, and every pure and wise spirit that ever took flesh. To be great is to be misunderstood.

19   *This journal entry in the summer of 1838 may well be the root of one of Emerson's most famous aphorisms, "Trust thyself; every heart resounds to that iron string."*

Forget the past. Be not the slave of your own past. In your prayer, in your teaching cumber not yourself with solicitude lest you contradict somewhat you have stated in this or that public place. So you worship the dull God Terminus & not the Lord of Lords. But dare rather to quit the platform, plunge into the sublime seas, dive deep, & swim far, so shall you come back with self-respect, with new power, with an advanced experience, that shall explain & overlook the old. Trust your emotion. If perchance you say in a metaphysical analysis I cannot concede personality to the Deity, yet when the devout motions of the soul

come, yield to them heart & soul if they should clothe
God with garments of shape and color.

20

Blind men in Rome complained that the streets were dark.
To the dull mind all nature is leaden. To the illuminated
mind the whole world burns and sparkles with light.

21

*In mid-June of 1836 Emerson had a particularly
moving experience in the woods around Walden
Pond. At one point he declared, "I love the wood
god. I love the mighty Pan." Though it is difficult
to imagine Emerson worshiping the Greek god of
fertility, it is clear that his connections with the
woods around him were intensely spiritual.*

Yesterday I walked in the storm. And truly in the fields I am
not alone or unacknowledged. They nod to me & I to them.
The waving of the boughs of trees in the storm is new to
me & old. It takes me by surprise & yet is not unknown.
Its effect is like that of a higher thought or a better emotion coming over me when I deemed I was thinking justly
or doing right. We distrust & deny inwardly our own sympathy with nature.

22

*The nature lover could also experience the irrita-
tions of the outdoors and engage in somewhat ludi-
crous ways of coping with them.*

An orientalist recommended to me who was a Hercules
among the bugs and curculios [weevils], a Persian exper-

iment of setting a lamp under the plum tree in a white-washed tub with a little water in it, by night. But the curculio showed no taste for so elegant a death. A few flies & harmless beetles perished, & one genuine Yankee spider instantly wove his threads across the tub, thinking that there was likely to be a crowd & he might as well set up his booth & win something for himself. At night in the garden all bugdom & flydom is abroad. This year is like Africa or New Holland, all surprising forms & masks of creeping, flying, & loathsomeness.

23   *FOREBEARANCE* [*sic*]

Hast thou named all the birds without a gun?
Loved the wood-rose and left it on its stalk?
At rich men's tables eaten bread and pulse?
Unarmed, faced danger with a heart of trust?
And loved so well a high behavior,
In man or maid, that thou from speech has
    refrained,
Nobility more nobly to repay?
O, be my friend and teach me to be thine!

24   *Bronson Alcott (father of Louisa May) was a dear friend of Emerson, a central figure in the Transcendental group and one of the original founders of "The Dial." He was an educator with progressive ideas, an eloquent orator, but never quite successful in most of his projects. Emerson was his emotional and sometime financial support for many years.*

Alcott has the great merit of being a believer in the soul. I think he has more faith in the Ideal than any man I have known. Hence his welcome influence. A wise woman said to me that he has few thoughts, too few. She could count them all. Books, conversation, discipline will give him more. But what were many thoughts if he had not this distinguishing Faith, which is a palpable proclamation out of the deeps of nature that God yet is? With many thoughts, & without this he would be only one more of a countless throng of lettered men; but now you cannot spare the fortification that he is.

25

To go into solitude, a man needs to retire as much from his chamber as from society. I am not solitary whilst I read and write, though nobody is with me. But if a man would be alone, let him look at the stars.

26

In Sanskrit, the word "Brahma" or "Brahman" means "The Supreme, second to none."

BRAHMA

If the red slayer think he slays,
    Or if the slain thinks he is slain,
They know not well the subtle ways
    I keep, and pass, and turn again.

Far or forgot to me is near;
    Shadow and the sunlight are the same;

The vanished gods to me appear;
    And one to me are shame and fame.

They reckon ill who leave me out;
    When me they fly, I am the wings;
I am the doubter and the doubt,
    And I the hymn the Brahmin sings.

The strong gods pine for my abode
    And pine in vain the sacred Seven;
But thou, meek lover of the good!
    Find me, and turn thy back on heaven.

27

Art is a jealous mistress, and if a man have a genius for painting, poetry, music, architecture or philosophy, he makes a bad husband and ill provider, and should be wise in season and not fetter himself with duties which will embitter his days and spoil him for his proper work. We had in this region, twenty years ago, among our educated men, a sort of Arcadian fanaticism, a passionate desire to go upon the land and unite farming to intellectual pursuits. Many effected their purpose and made the experiment, and some became downright ploughmen, but all were cured of their faith that scholarship and practical farming (I mean, with one's own hands) could be united.

 This is the kind of Emersonian passage that may have inspired his friend Horace Greeley to exhort young men from New England to "Go West!"

The world – this shadow of the soul, or other me, lies

wide around. Its attractions are the keys which unlock my thoughts and make me acquainted with myself. I run eagerly into this resounding tumult. I grasp the hands of those next to me, and take my place in the ring to suffer and to work, taught by an instinct that so shall the dumb abyss be vocal with speech. I pierce its order; I dissipate its fear; I dispose of it within the circuit of my expanding life. So much only of life as I know by experience, so much of the wilderness have I vanquished and planted, or so far have I extended my being, my dominion. I do not see how any man can afford, for the sake of his nerves and his nap, to spare any action which he can partake. It is pearls and rubies to his discourse. Drudgery, calamity, exasperation, want, are instructors in eloquence and wisdom.

29 *Lest we believe that Emerson's idealism carries him beyond the world's reality this eloquent celebration of Matter should correct the impression.*

Today at the cliff we held our *villeggiatura* [county gathering]. I saw nothing better than the passage of the river by the dark clump of trees that lined the bank in one spot for a short distance. There nature charmed the eye with her distinct & perfect painting. As the flowing silver reached that point, it darkened, & yet every wave celebrated its passage through the shade by one sparkle. But ever the direction of the sparkles was onward, onward. No one receded. At one invariable pace like marchers in a procession to solemn music, in perfect time, in perfect order they moved onward, onward & I saw the Warning of their eternal flow. Then the rock seemed good to me. I think we can never afford to part with Matter. How dear & beautiful it is to us!

As water to our thirst, so is this rock to our eyes & hands & feet. It is firm water; it is cold flame. What refreshment, what health, what magic affinity! ever an old friend, ever like a dear friend or brother when we chat affectedly with strangers, come in this honest face whilst we prattle with men & takes a grave liberty with us & shames us out of our nonsense.

30 *Emerson, the modern man, promotes "doing your own thing" some one hundred years before the Age of Aquarius.*

Reform. The objection to conforming to usages that have become dead to you, is that it scatters your force: loses your time, blears the impression of your character. If you maintain the church, join the bible society, vote with the Whig or Government party, spread your table like other housekeepers, under all these screens I have difficulty to detect the precise man you are. Do your thing & I shall know you.

· J U L Y ·

1

'Twas one of the charmed days
　　When the Genius of God doth flow,
The wind may alter twenty ways,
　　A tempest cannot blow;
It may blow north, it still is warm:
　　Or south it still is clear;
Or east it smells like a clover-farm;
　　Or west no thunder fear.

2

There is a limit to the effect of written eloquence. It may do much, but the miracles of eloquence can only be expected from the man who thinks on his legs; he who thinks may thunder; on him the Holy Ghost may fall & from him pass.

3

In a letter to an unnamed correspondent, Emerson states as clearly as he has anywhere his core belief. His statement that his "creed is goodness" is similar to the statement made by the Dalai Lama in a letter to the public in 2001, immediately following the events of September 11th: "My religion is kindness."

I am very much moved by the earnestness of your appeal, but very much humbled by it; for in attributing to me that attainment & that rest wh. [*sic*] I know well are not mine, it accuses my shortcomings. I am, like you, the seeker of the perfect & admirable Good. My creed is very simple; that Goodness is the only Reality; that Goodness alone can we trust: to that we may trust all & always: beautiful

& blessed & blessing is it, even though it should seem to slay me. Beyond this, I have no knowledge, no intelligence of methods; I know no steps, no degrees, no favorite means, no detached rules. Itself is gate & road & leader & march. Only trust it; be of it, be it — & it shall be well with us forever. It will be & govern in its own transcendent way, & not in ways that Arithmatic [*sic*] & mortal experience can measure. I can surely give no account of the origin & growth of my trust, but this only: that the trust accompanies the incoming of that which is trusted. Blessed be that! Happy am I when I am a trust; unhappy & so far dead if it should ebb from me.

 One of Emerson's most famous poems, this hymn was sung at the completion of the battle monument in Concord, on April 19th, 1837.

CONCORD HYMN

By the rude bridge that arched the flood,
    Their flag to April's breeze unfurled,
Here once the embattled farmers stood,
    And fired the shot heard round the world.

The foe long since in silence slept;
    Alike the conqueror silent sleeps;
And Time the ruined bridge has swept
    Down the dark stream which seaward creeps.

On this green bank, by this soft stream,
    We set today a votive stone;
That memory may their dead redeem,
    When, like our sires, our sons are gone.

Spirit, that made those heroes dare
        To die, and leave their children free,
Bid Time and Nature gently spare
        The shaft we raise to them and thee.

5 *Emerson based his poem "Hamatreya" on a pas-*
sage in one of the Hindu texts he read many times.
The original, "Vishnu Purana," was a fable about
princes who are inflated with their possessions;
Emerson found it easy to adapt the theme with the
names of long-established landowners in the
Concord area. The reply of the earth to the human
presumption is included in the poem as "Earth-
Song." (See October 2.)

HAMATREYA

Bulkeley, Hunt, Willard, Hosmer, Meriam, Flint,
Possessed the land which rendered to their toil
Hay, corn, roots, hemp, flax, apples, wool and wood.
Each of these landlords walked amidst his farm,
Saying, "'Tis mine, my children's, and my name's.
How sweet the west wind sounds in my own trees!
How graceful climb those shadows on my hill!
I fancy the pure waters and the flags
Know me, as does my dog: we sympathize;
And, I affirm, my actions smack of the soil."

Where are these men? Asleep beneath their
        grounds:
And strangers, fond as they, their furrows plough.
Earth laughs in flowers, to see her boastful boys

Earth-proud, proud of the earth which is not
    theirs;
Who steer the plough, but cannot steer their feet
Clear of the grave.

6   *Emerson was fond of the mountains of New Hamp-*
   shire, and on a visit to Conway, among the White
   Mountains, he was inspired to define religious
   belief and practice in very specific terms.

Here, among the mountains, the pinions of thought should
be strong, and one should see the errors of men from
calmer height of love and wisdom. What is the message
that is given to me to communicate next Sunday? Religion
in the mind is not credulity, and in the practice is not form.
It is a life. It is the order and soundness of a man. It is not
something *to be got*, to be *added*, but is a new life of those
faculties you have. It is to do right. It is to love, it is to
serve, it is to think, it is to be humble.

7   *Here Emerson expands on Plato's concept of the*
   "Universal Soul" and includes in it a psychic
   potential that is immensely powerful, but difficult
   to galvanize into action.

The generic soul in each individual is a giant overcome
with sleep which locks up almost all his senses, & only
leaves him a little superficial animation Once in an age, at
hearing some deeper voice, he lifts his iron lids, & his eyes
pierce through all appearances, & his tongue tells what
shall be in the latest times: then he is obeyed like a God,
but quickly the lids fall, & sleep returns.

Written a year before the previous entry, in this meditation on the exalted nature of being human, Emerson is showing in other ways the influence of Plato (and the Vedanta texts) on his ideas about the qualities of the human spirit.

A certain wandering light comes to me which I instantly perceive to the Cause of Causes. It transcends all proving. It is itself the ground of being; and I see that it is not one & I another, but this is the life of my life. That is one fact, then; that in certain moments I have known that I existed directly from God, and am, as it were, his organ. And in my ultimate consciousness Am He. The secondly, the contradictory fact is familiar, that I am a surprised spectator & learner of all my life. This is the habitual posture of the mind, – beholding. But whenever the day dawns, the great day of truth on the soul, it comes with an awful invitation to me to accept it, to blend with its aurora.

Emerson the literary critic/tutor could be blunt in his review of his friends' work. But he was faithful to his own principles and "took time to be civil."

Dear Miss Lazarus,

I ought long ago to have taken a decided part either to work out my criticism on your poems – as I doubted not at first to do, – or to send them back, & committed them to your own. But I still believed that my preoccupations were temporary, & the freedom would presently return – which does not return. . . . For Admetus, I had fully intended to use your consent & carry it to Mr. Fields for the "Atlantic." But on reading it more carefully, I found that what had so strongly impressed me on the first reading was the dignity and pathos of the story as you have told it, which still charms me. But the execution in details is not equal to this merit or to the need. You permit feeble lines & feeble words. Thus you write words which you can never have spoken. Please now to articulate the word "smileless," – which you have used twice at no long intervals. You must cut out all the lines and words you can spare & thus add force. . . . I have kept the poem so long that you will have forgotten it much, & will read it with fresh eyes. . . . Cut down everything that does not delight you to the least possible. I have marked a few heedless words. "Doubt" does not "ravage" nor be "revenged."

10   *LINES TO ELLEN*

Tell me, maiden, dost thou use
Thyself thro' Nature to diffuse?
All the angles of the coast
Were tenanted by thy sweet ghost,
Bore thy colors every flower.
Thine each leaf and berry bore;
All wore thy badges and thy favors
In their scent or in their savors,
Every moth with painted wing,
Every bird is carolling
The wood-boughs with thy manners, waved,
The rocks uphold thy name engraved,
The sod throbbed friendly to my feet
And the sweet air with thee was sweet.

11 *In this particular journal entry we must not read Emerson as being concerned with a person's "public reputation," but rather see the words "any body" as "his own man."*

Society is babyish. Talleyrand's question is the main one to be asked; not, is he honest? is he rich? is he committed? is he of the movement, or, is he of the establishment? But, "is he any body?" We want fire; a little less mutton and a little more genius.

12 *In this statement Emerson seems to anticipate Charles Darwin's theory of evolution, which was yet to be propounded. The Darwin he refers to here is Erasmus, Charles's grandfather, and Emerson's contemporary. Emerson coined a phrase – arrested and progressive development – which has become standard in modern psychology and sociology. Research has shown that John Hunter did not, in fact, use it.*

The electric word pronounced by John Hunter 100 years ago, *arrested and progressive development,* indicating the way upward from the invisible protoplasm to the highest organism, gave the poetic key to Natural Science, of which the theories of Geoffroy Saint-Hilaire, of Oken, of Goethe, of Agassiz and Owen and Darwin in zoology, and botany, are the fruits, – a hint whose power is not yet exhausted, showing unity and perfect order in physics.

13 *The previous quotation was written in 1854. The following text, written eighteen years earlier, helps*

us understand what made Emerson so visionary
about the natural sciences. The personal phenom-
ena that he describes would be familiar to Native
Americans of every era.

The universe is a more of an amazing puzzle than ever, as you glance along this bewildering series of animated forms, – the hazy butterflies, the carved shells, the birds, beasts, fishes, insects, snakes, and the upheaving principle of life everywhere incipient, in the very rock aping organized forms. Not a form so grotesque, so savage, nor so beautiful but is an expression of some property inherent in man the observer, – an occult relation between the very scorpions and man. I feel the centipede in me, – cayman, carp, eagle, and fox. I am moved by strange sympathies; I say continually "I will be a naturalist."

14 *The key word in the following text is clearly "saint-ly." The rest of us still have to watch our diet.*

It makes no difference what a saintly soul eats or drinks; let him eat venison or roots, let him drink champagne or water, nothing will harm him or intoxicate or impoverish him: he eats as though he eat not, & drinks as though he drank not. But we are Skeptics at our dinner table & therefore our food is noxious & our bodies fat or lean. Looking as we do at means, & not at grand ends, being in our action disunited, our bodies have come to be detached also from our souls, & we speak of our health.

15 *Though he had resigned his own pastorate in 1832, Emerson was invited to speak by the stu-*

dents of the Harvard Divinity School, from which he himself was graduated in 1829. On Sunday, July 15th, 1837, he gave a talk that castigated the contemporary Unitarian clergy for irrelevance and for focusing on a personal god, criticisms that would earn Emerson widespread wrath among his fellow pastors. But he did establish the cornerstone of his principle that God is in the "divine nature" of even blind matter and lies most certainly in the heart of the humblest man.

The world is not the product of manifold power, but of one will, of one mind; and that one mind is everywhere active, in each ray of the star, in each wavelet of the pool; and whatever opposes that will is everywhere balked and baffled, because things are made so, and not otherwise. Good is positive, Evil is merely privative, not absolute: it is like cold, which is the privation of heat. All evil is so much death or nonentity. Benevolence is absolute and real. So much benevolence as a man hath, so much life hath he. For all things proceed out of this same spirit, which is differently named love, justice, temperance, in its different applications, just as the ocean receives different names on the several shores on which it washes. All things proceed out of the same spirit, and all things conspire with it. Whilst a man seeks good ends, he is strong by the whole strength of nature. Insofar as he roves from these ends, he bereaves himself of power, or auxiliaries; his being shrinks out of all remote channels, he becomes less and less, a mote, a point, until absolute badness is absolute death.

16

Men are in all ways better than they seem. They like flattery for the moment, but they know the truth for their own. It is a foolish cowardice which keeps us from trusting them and speaking to them rude truth. They resent your honesty for an instant, they will thank you for it always. What is it we heartily wish of each other? Is it to be pleased and flattered? No, but to be convicted and exposed, to be shamed out of our nonsense of all kinds, and made men of, instead of ghosts and phantoms. We are weary of gliding ghostlike through the world, which is itself so slight and unreal. We crave a sense of reality, though it comes in strokes of pain.

17

In his correspondence with the women he held dearest, (Caroline Sturgis and Margaret Fuller, in particular) Emerson seems compelled repeatedly to review and define the "laws of friendship."

I hate everything frugal and cowardly in friendship. *That*, at least should be brave and generous. When we fear the withdrawal of love from ourselves by the new relations which our companions must form, it is mere infidelity. We believe in our eyes and not in the Creator. We do not see any equal pretender in the field, and we conclude that Beauty and Virtue must vail their high top, and buy their Eden by the loss of that which makes them ours. But we are wiser with the next sun, and know that a true and *native* friend is only the extension of our own being and perceiving into other skies and societies, there learning wisdom, there discerning spirits, and attracting our own for us, as truly as we had done hitherto in our strait enclosure. I wish you to go out on an adventurous missionary, into all nations of happy souls, and by all whom you can greatly and by any whom you can wholly love, I see that I too must be immeasurably enriched.

18 *He confesses his love of "strolling" and thinks it makes him a sluggard, or at least odd.*

It is a peculiarity (I find upon observation of others) of humor in me, my strong propensity for strolling. I deliberately shut up my books in a cloudy July noon, put on my old clothes and old hat and slink away to the whortleberry bushes and slip with the greatest satisfaction into a little cowpath where I am sure I can defy observation. This point gained, I solace myself for hours with picking blueberries and other trash of the woods, far from fame, behind the birch-trees. I remember them in winter, I expect them in spring. I do not know a creature that I think has the same humor, or would think it respectable.

19

I find it a great and fatal difference whether I court the muse, or the muse courts me. That is the ugly disparity between age and youth.

20 *Though he is only sixty-one, Emerson muses on the benefits of the "golden years."*

Old age brings along with its uglinesses the comfort that you will soon be out of it, – which ought to be a substantial relief to such discontented pendulums as we are. To be out of the war, out of debt, out of the drouth, out of the blues, out of the dentist's hands, out of the second thoughts, mortifications, and remorses that inflict such twinges and shooting pains, – out of the next winter, and the high prices, and company below your ambition, – surely these are soothing hints. And, harbinger of this, what an alleviator is sleep, which muzzles all these dogs for me every day?

21 *No author could have wished for a better send-off for his first book of poems than the one Mr. Walter Whitman of Brooklyn, New York, received in 1855 from R. W. Emerson of Concord, Massachusetts.*

Dear Sir,

I am not blind to the worth of the wonderful gift of "Leaves of Grass." I find it the most extraordinary piece of wit & wisdom that America has yet contributed. I am very happy in reading it, as great power makes us happy. It meets the demand I am always making of what seemed the sterile & stingy nature, as if too much handiwork or too much lymph in the temperament were making our western wits fat & mean. I give you joy of your free & brave thought. I have great joy in it. I find incomparable things said incomparably well, as they must be. I find the courage of treatment, which so delights us, & which large perception only can inspire. I greet you at the beginning of a great career, which yet must have had a long foreground somewhere for such a start. I rubbed my eyes a little to see if this sunbeam were no illusion; but the solid sense of the book is a solid certainty. It has the best merits namely, of fortifying and encouraging.

I did not know until I, last night, saw the book advertised in the newspaper, that I could trust the name as real & available for a post office. I wish to see my benefactor, & have felt much like striking my tasks, & visiting New York to pay you my respects.

22 *Once again, in the spirit of balance and "compensation," Emerson urges us to give the "work of our hands" a respect equal to that achieved by our minds.*

A man should have a farm or a mechanical craft for his culture. We must have a basis for our higher accomplishments, our delicate entertainments of poetry and philosophy in the work of our hands. We must have an antagonism in the tough world for all the variety of our spiritual faculties, or they will not be born. Manual labor is the study of the external world. The advantage of riches remains with him who procured them, not with the heir. When I go into the garden with a spade, and dig a bed, I feel such an exhilaration and health that I discover that I have been defrauding myself all this time in letting others do for me what I should have done with my own hands. But not only health, but education is in the work. It is possible that I, who get indefinite quantities of sugar, hominy, cotton, buckets, cookery-ware, and letter-paper, by simply signing my name once in three months to a check in favor for John Smith & Co, traders, get the fair share of exercise to my faculties by that act which nature intended for me in making all these far-fetched matters important to my comfort.

23 *Emerson provides some timeless thoughts about the distinctions between conservatives and radicals.*

Is not every man sometimes a radical in politics? Men are conservatives when they are least vigorous, or when they are most luxurious. They are conservatives after dinner, or before taking their rest; when they are sick, or aged: in the morning, or when their intellect or their conscience has been aroused; when they hear music, or when they read poetry, they are radicals. In the circle of the rankest Tories that could be collected in England, Old or New, let a powerful and stimulating intellect, a man of great heart and mind act on them, and very quickly these frozen conservators will yield to the friendly influence, these hopeless will begin to hope, these haters will begin to love, these immovable statues will begin to spin and revolve.

24 *Emerson's address at Dartmouth College on July 24, 1838, is considered by many scholars to be a lower-keyed version of his Harvard Divinity School address, but it lacks none of the fervor or confidence that the great lecturer exhibited when he exhorted young ministers-to-be.*

A man of cultivated mind, but reserved habits, sitting silent, admires the miracle of free, impassioned, picturesque speech, in the man addressing an assembly – a state of being and power, how unlike his own! Presently his own emotion rises to his lips, and overflows in speech. He must also rise and say somewhat. Once embarked, once having overcome the novelty of the situation, he finds it just as easy and natural to speak – to speak with thoughts, with pictures, with rhythmical balance of sentences – as it was to sit silent; for, it needs not to do, but to suffer; he only adjusts himself to the free spirit which gladly utters itself through him; and motion is as easy as rest.

25

To the attentive eye, each moment of the year has its own beauty, and in the same field, it beholds every hour, a picture which was never seen before, and which shall never be seen again.

26

I often hear the remark made that there is great pleasure in giving up all care, when we find that we are really sick. And one wishes for a good fit of dyspepsia or hemorrhage to procure him leisure & freedom. Is this a trait of New England in Eighteen-hundred-forty-dom [*sic*], or should I have found the same satire on daily life in Rome & in Thebes?

27   *BERRYING*

> May be true what I had heard,–
> 'Earth's a howling wilderness,
> Truculent with fraud and force.'
> Said I, strolling through the pastures,
> And along the river-side.
> Caught among the blackberry vines,

Feeding on the Ethiops sweet,
Pleasant fancies overtook me.
I said, 'What influence me preferred,
Elect, to dreams thus beautiful?'
The vines replied, 'And didst thou dream
No wisdom from our berries went?'

 Emerson applies the rules of what we now know as ecology to point up how inescapable it is that our knowledge is built on those who have gone before. (And this from the man who also wrote, "I hate quotations. Tell me what you know.")

It is inevitable that you are indebted to the past. You are fed and formed by it. The old forest is decomposed for the composition of the new forest. The old animals have given their bodies to the earth to furnish through chemistry the forming race, and every individual is only a momentary fixation of what was yesterday another's, is to-day his, and will belong to a third to-morrow. So it is in thought. Our knowledge is the amassed thought and experience of innumerable minds; our language, our science, all religion, our opinions, our fancies we inherited. . . . Our country, customs, laws, our ambitions, and our notions of fit and fair, – all these we never made; we found them ready-made; we but quote them.

29

Old age begins in the nursery, and before the young American is put into a jacket and trousers, he says, "I want something which I never saw before," and, "I wish I was not I."

30 *Deceptively simple and hypnotically rhythmic, Emerson's poem, "The Sphinx," is the poet mocking himself as a philosopher, since the Sphinx counters all his Transcendental theories and, at the end of the poem, consumes him.*

THE SPHINX

The fate of the man-child,
    The meaning of man,
Known fruit of the unknown,
    Daedalian plan,
Out of sleeping a waking,
    Out of waking a sleep;
Life death overtaking;
    Deep underneath deep.

31 *Obviously, the strongest influence of Eastern thought on Emerson is the Hindu tradition, given his deep involvement with Vedantic texts and the* Bhagavad Gita, *but he certainly can think and sound remarkably like Lao-Tse enunciating the principles of yin and yang polarities in the* Tao Te Ching.

That great principle of Undulation in nature, that shows itself in the inspiring and expiring of the breath; in desire and satiety, in the ebb and flow of the sea; in day and night; in heat and cold; and as yet more deeply ingrained in every atom and every fluid, is known to us under the name of Polarity – these "fits of easy transmission and reflection," as Newton called them – are the law of nature because they are the law of spirit.

·AUGUST·

1   *The Anti-Slavery Society women of twelve of the
towns surrounding Concord asked Emerson to give
a speech on the tenth anniversary of the emancipation by England of the negroes in the British West
Indies. After much difficulty in securing a venue
for the meeting (the slavery issue was still very
debatable at that time, even in Massachusetts)
Emerson delivered his address in the courthouse to
a packed auditorium.*

The First of August marks the entrance of a new element
into modern politics, namely, the civilization of the negro.
A man is added to the human family. Not the least affecting part of this history of abolition, is the annihilation of
the old indecent nonsense about the nature of the negro . . .
the emancipation is observed, in the Islands, to have
wrought for the negro a benefit as sudden as when a ther-
mometer is brought out of the shade into the sun. It has
given him eyes and ears. . . . He is now the principal, if not
the only mechanic, in the West Indies; and is, besides, an
architect, a physician, a lawyer, a magistrate, an editor, and
a valued and increasing political power . . . the sentiment of
Right, once very low and indistinct, but ever more articulate, because it is the voice of the universe, pronounces
Freedom. The Power that built this fabric of things affirms
it in the heart; and in the history of the First of August,
has made a sign to the ages, of his will.

2   *In a letter to his Aunt Mary Moody, written from
Rome when he was thirty, Emerson described his
vision (perhaps the universal vision) of the person
who would be a true teacher.*

God's greatest gift is a teacher & when will he send me one, full of truth & boundless benevolence & heroic sentiments. I can describe the man, & have done so already in prose and verse. I know the idea well, but where is its real blood warm counterpart. . . . I may as well set down what our stern experience replies with the tongue of all its days. Son of man, it saith, all giving & receiving is reciprocal; you entertain angels unawares, but they cannot impart more or higher things than you are in a state to receive. But every step of your progress affects the intercourse you hold with all others; elevates its tone, deepens its meaning, sanctifies its spirit, and when time & suffering & selfdenial [*sic*] shall have transformed and glorified this spotted self, you shall find your fellows also transformed & their faces shall shine upon you with the light of wisdom & the beauty of holiness.

 One of the famous quatrains that Emerson wrote in 1863 in praise of Northern soldiers continues to be quoted today.

So nigh is grandeur to our dust
So near is God to man,
When Duty whispers low, *Thou must,*
The youth replies, *I can.*

 In this letter he writes in 1861 to a friend – James Elliot Cabot, who would later become one of Emerson's biographers – Emerson's patriotism and hatred of slavery overcomes his aversion to war.

My dear Cabot,
   I was very glad yesterday to hear from you, & on such

high matters. The war – though from such despicable beginnings, has assumed such huge proportions that it threatens to engulf us all – no pre-occupation can exclude it, & no hermitage hide us. – And yet, gulf as it is, the war with its defeats & uncertainties is immensely better than what we lately called the integrity of the Republic, as amputation is better than cancer. I think we are all agreed in this, and find it out by wondering why we are so pleased, though so beaten & so poor. No matter how low down, if not in false position. If the abundance of heaven only sends us a fair share of light & conscience, we shall redeem America for all its sinful years since the century began.

5 *In the second part of his poem, "Woodnotes," Emerson has the pine tree sing some of the thoughts and sentiments he has expressed in various essays, as well as in some of his earlier lectures on science. The idea of the creation of the world contained in these lines is suggestive of both the "Big Bang" theory and the doctrine of pantheism.*

Halteth never in one shape,
But forever doth escape,
Like wave of flame, into new forms
Of gem, and air, of plants, and worms
I, that to-day am a pine,
Yesterday was a bundle of grass.

6 *Once again, Emerson miscalculates his popularity. But he would not have altered a thing to reverse what he thought was public opionion.*

I observe that all bookish men have a tendency to believe they are unpopular. [Theodore] Parker gravely informs me by word and by letter that he is precisely the most unpopular man in New England. [Bronson] Alcott believed the same thing of himself, and I, no doubt, if they had not anticipated me in claiming this distinction, should have claimed it for myself.

7

Every revolution was first a thought in one man's mind and when the same thought occurs to another man, it is the key to that era.

8

In his essay, "Domestic Life," Emerson delivers some provocative thoughts on both the definition and the impermanence of beauty.

Every individual nature has its own beauty. One is struck in every company, at every fireside, with the riches of Nature, when he hears as many new tones, all musical, sees in each person original manners, which have a proper and peculiar charm, and reads new expression of face. He perceives that Nature has laid for each the foundations of the divine building, if the soul will build thereon. There is no face, or form, which one cannot in fancy associate with great power of intellect or with generosity of soul. In our experience, to be sure, beauty is not, as it ought to be, the dower of man and of woman as invariably as sensation. Beauty is, even in the beautiful, occasional, – or, as one has said, culminating and perfect only a single moment before which it is unripe, and after which it is on the wane. But beauty is never quite absent from our eyes. Every face, every figure suggests its own right and sound estate.

9   *Given his radical ideas on how to appoint college professors, one wonders where Emerson would have stood on the issue of tenure.*

The teacher should be the complement of the pupil, now for the most part they are earth's diameters wide of each other. The college professor should be elected by setting all the candidates loose on a miscellaneous gang of young men taken at large from the street. He who could get the ear of these youths after a certain number of hours, or of the greatest number of these youths, should be professor. Let him see if he could interest these rowdy boys in the meaning of a list of words.

10   *Emerson expresses some wistful thoughts about the general public's resistance to the principle of universalism that sits at the heart of his transcendental philosophy. (He also proffers an uncharacteristically snide comment about women.)*

A newspaper in Providence contains some notice of Transcendentalism, & deplores Mr. Emerson's doctrine that the argument for immortality betrays weakness. The piece seems to be written by a woman. It begins with round sentences but ends in Oh's & Ah's. Yet cannot society apprehend the doctrine of One Mind? Can we not satisfy ourselves with the fact of living for the Universe, of lodging our beatitude therein? Patriotism has been thought great in Sparta, in Rome, in New England even, only sixty years ago. How long before Universalism or Humanity shall be credible & beautiful?

11 *In the middle of an address on "The Method of Nature," Emerson proposes a definition of love. (See also "Give All to Love" on February 14th.)*

What is Love, and why is it the chief good, but because it is an overpowering enthusiasm? Never self-possessed or prudent, it is all abandonment. Is it not a certain admirable wisdom, preferable to all other advantages, and whereof all others are only secondary ... because this is that in which the individual is no longer his own foolish master, but inhales an odorous and celestial air, is wrapped around with awe of the object, blending for the time that object with the real and only good, and consults every omen in nature with tremulous interest. When we speak truly – is not he only unhappy who is not in love? his fancied free-dom and self-rule – is it not so much death? He who is in love is wise and becoming wiser, sees newly every time he looks at the object beloved, drawing from it with his eyes and mind those virtues which it possesses. Therefore if the object be not itself a living and expanding soul, he presently exhausts it. But the love remains in his mind, and the wisdom it brought him; and it craves a newer and higher object.

12 *Emerson is only twenty-four years old, but he has rather definite ideas about how people behave in private after they have shed their public personal-ities at the end of the day.*

He takes off his goodness like a cumbersome garment and grows silent and splenetic. He has got rid of the prepossessing elegance of his address, that buoyant alacrity in the offices of politeness that won your praise.

He is intemperate at his table; he is a sluggard in bed; he is slothful and useless in his chair; he is sour or false in conversation. He breaks the commandments because he is at home. A strange reason surely for license and vice! Will the curtains of his window shroud him from the Omniscient Eye? When we need the stimulus of a great occasion and many observers to excite our virtue, what is in effect but to say that we fear man more than God and respect men more than we respect ourselves?

13

I have seen in the sky a chain of summer lightning which at once showed to me that the Greeks drew from nature when they painted the thunderbolt in the hand of Jove.

14

It would be hard to find a passage from Emerson's writing that presents a stronger or clearer statement of his central teaching.

A little consideration of what takes place around us every day would show us that a higher law than that of our will regulates events; that our painful labors are unnecessary and fruitless, that only in our easy, simple, spontaneous action are we strong, and by contenting ourselves with obedience we become divine. Belief and love, – a believing love will relieve us of a vast load of care. O my brothers, God exists. There is a soul at the center of nature and over the will of every man, so that none of us can harm the universe. It has so infused its strong attachment into nature that we prosper when we accept its advice, and when we struggle to wound its creatures our hands are glued to our sides, or they beat their own breasts. The whole course of things goes to teach us faith. We need only obey. There is guidance for each of us, and by lowly listening we shall hear the right word.

15   *Emerson understands that poets may be given to using stimulant substances, but he is quite clear about what he conceives to be the "true nectar."*

This is the reason why bards love wine, mead, narcotics, coffee, tea, opium, the fumes of sandalwood and tobacco, or whatever other procurers of animal exhilaration. All men avail themselves of such means as they can, to add this extraordinary power to their normal powers; and to this end they prize conversation, music, pictures, sculpture, dancing, theatres, travelling, war, mobs, fires, gaming, politics, or love, or science, or animal intoxication – which are several coarser or finer *quasi*-mechanical substitutes for the true nectar, which is the ravishment of the intellect by coming nearer to the fact.

16   *"Ode," inscribed to W. H. Channing, a Transcendentalist friend of Emerson's, is concerned with American history and Emerson's feelings about some of the issues of his time. The most satirical part is aimed at Daniel Webster, who had been a friend of the Emerson family and a hero of Waldo's for many years, but who now, in his willingness to*

tolerate slavery for the sake of preserving the Union,
has incurred Emerson's bitter opposition.

The god who made New Hampshire
Taunted the lofty land
With little men;
Small bat and wren
House in the oak:
If the earth-fire cleave
The upheaved land, and bury the folk,
The southern crocodile would grieve.
Virtue palters; Right is hence;
Freedom praised, but hid;
Funeral eloquence
Rattles the coffin-lid.

17 *Emerson, as a transcendentalist, was fascinated by
Hindu and other eastern texts and sees clearly the
connection between Plato's ideas and many prem-
ises of Asiatic philosophies.*

Meanwhile, Plato in Egypt and in eastern pilgrimages,
imbibed the idea of one Deity, in which all things are ab-
sorbed. The unity of Asia and the detail of Europe; the in-
finitude of the Asiatic soul and the defining, result-loving,
machine-making, surface-seeking, opera-going Europe, –
Plato came to join, and by contact to enhance the energy
of each. The excellence of Europe and Asia are in his brain.
Metaphysics and natural philosophy expressed the genius
of Europe; he substructs the religion of Asia, as the base.

18

The sun shines and warms and lights us and we have no curiosity to know why this is so; but we ask the reason of all evil, of pain, of hunger, and musquitoes [*sic*] and silly people.

19

Trust thyself: every heart vibrates to that iron string.

Emerson, aware that his memory is failing, writes one of his last letters to his oldest friend, William Henry Furness, who was a year older than he.

Ellen asks me what message I wish to send to you. I tell her immortal love, & the gladness that though you count more months than I you have not & shall not like me lose the names, when you wish to call them, of your contemporary or antecedent friends & teachers.

Emerson urges "man thinking" to remain independent at all costs of the people and events that surround him.

These being his functions, it becomes him [the scholar] to feel all confidence in himself and to defer never to the popular cry. He and he only knows the world. The world of any moment is the merest appearance. Some great decorum, some fetish of a government, some ephemeral trade, or war, or man, is cried up by half mankind and cried down by the other half, as if all depended on this particular up or down. The odds are the whole question is not worth the poorest thought which the scholar has lost in listening to the controversy. Let him not quit his belief that a popgun is a popgun, though the ancient and honorable of the earth affirm it to be the crack of doom. In silence, in steadiness, in severe abstraction, let him hold by himself; add observation to observation, patient of neglect, patient of reproach, and bide his own time – happy enough if he can satisfy himself alone that this day he has seen something truly.

22

Meek young men grow up in libraries, believing it their duty to accept the views which Cicero, which Locke, which Bacon, have given; forgetful that Cicero, Locke, and Bacon were only young men in libraries when they wrote these books.

23

Society is a joint-stock company, in which the members agree, for the better securing of his bread to each shareholder, to surrender the liberty and culture of the eater.

24

It appears that in August of 1859 medical opinions were as disparate as they are in our own day.

One Wrong Step. On Wachusett, I sprained my foot. It was slow to heal, and I went to the doctors. Dr. Henry Bigelow said, "Splint and absolute rest." Dr. Russell said, "Rest, yes; but a splint, no." Dr. Bartlett said, "Neither splint nor rest, but go and walk." Dr. Russell said, "Pour water on the foot, but it must be warm." Dr. Jackson said, "Stand in a trout brook all day."

25

When I attended church, and the man in the pulpit was all clay and not of tuneable metal, I thought that if men would avoid that general language and general manner in which they strive to hide all that is peculiar, and would say only what was uppermost in their own minds, after their own individual manner, every man would be interesting.

26 *He pays his respects to the earthy origins of English drama.*

The playhouse was low enough to have entire interest for them; they were proprietors; it was low & popular; and not literary. That the scholar scorned it, was its saving essence. Shakespeare evidently thought the mass of old plays or of stage plays *corpus vile*, in which any experiment might be freely tried. Had the prestige which hedges about a modern tragedy or other worthless literary work existed, nothing could have been done. The coarse but warm blood of the living England circulated in the play as in street ballads, & gave body to his airy & majestic fancy. For the poet peremptorily needs a basis which he cannot supply; a tough chaos-deep soil, or main, or continent, on which his art may work, as the sculptor a block of stone, and this basis the popular mind supplies: otherwise all his flowers & elegances are transcendental and mere nuisance.

27

Emerson has some definite ideas about manners, and some refreshing notions about what we might learn from the forthrightness of animals.

In the points of good breeding, what I most require & insist upon is deference. I like that every chair should be a throne & hold a king. And what I most dislike is a low sympathy of each with his neighbor's palate & belly at table, anticipating without words what he wishes to eat & drink. If you wish bread, ask me for bread, & if you wish anchovies or lobster, ask me for them, & do not hold out your plate as if I knew already.

I respect cats, they seem to have so much else in their heads besides their mess. Yet every natural function can be dignified by deliberation & privacy. I prefer a tendency to stateliness to an excess of fellowship. In all things I would have the island of man inviolate. No degree of affection is to invade this religion. Lovers should guard their strangeness. As soon as they surrender that, they are no more lovers.

28

Emerson has some waspish observations on other people's householding.

H[enry] T[horeau] sturdily pushes his economy into houses & thinks it is the false mark of the gentleman that he is to pay much for his food. He ought to pay little for his food. Ice – he must have ice! And it is true, that, for each artificial want that can be invented & added to the ponderous expense, there is new clapping of hands of newspaper editors, & the donkey public. To put one more rock to be lifted betwixt a man & his true ends. If Socrates were here,

we could go & talk with him; but Longfellow, we cannot go
& talk with; there is a palace, & servants, & a row of bottles
of different coloured wines, & wine glasses, & fine coats.

29 *Emerson declared that everyday life, lived within a diverse population, provides the best education we can obtain.*

Life is our dictionary. Years are well spent in country
labors; in town; in insight into trades and manufactures; in
frank intercourse with many men and women; in science;
in art; to the one end of mastering in all their facts a language by which to illustrate and embody our perceptions.
I learn immediately from any speaker how much he has
already lived, through the poverty or the splendor of his
speech. Life lies behind us as the quarry from whence we
get tiles and copestones for the masonry of today. This is
the way to learn grammar. Colleges and books only copy
the language which the field and the work-yard made.

30

Whenever a mind is simple, and receives a divine wisdom,
old things pass away, – means, teachers, texts, temples,
fall; it lives now, and absorbs past and future into the present hour.

31 *At the age of thirty-five, Emerson is already a good example of his own definition of the self-reliant man and reassures himself that he knows his true vocation.*

Society has no bribe for me, neither in politics, nor church, nor college, nor city. My resources are far from exhausted. If they will not hear me lecture, I shall have leisure for my book which wants me. Beside, it is as a universal maxim worthy of all acceptation that a man may have that allowance which he takes. Take the place & attitude to which you see your unquestionable right, & all men acquiesce. Who are these murmerers [*sic*], these haters, these revilers? Men of no knowledge, & therefore no stability. The scholar on the contrary is sure of his point, is fast-rooted, & can surely predict the hour when all this roaring multitude shall roar for him. Analyze the chiding opposition & it is made up of such timidities, uncertainties, & no opinions, that it is not worth dispersing.

·SEPTEMBER·

1

Fairest, choose the fairest members
   Of our lithe society;
June's glories and September's
   Show our love and piety.

2

*In his famous essay, "The Over-Soul," Emerson
seems to suggest that what we call meditation is
one of the paths to the Universal Mind.*

Let man, then, learn the revelation of all nature and all
thought to his heart; this, namely; that the Highest dwells
with him; that the sources of nature are in his own mind,
if the sentiment of duty is there. But if he would know
what the great God speaketh, he must "go into his closet
and shut the door," as Jesus said. God will not make himself manifest to cowards. He must greatly listen to himself,
withdrawing himself from all the accents of other men's
devotion. Even their prayers are hurtful to him, until he
have made his own. Our religion vulgarly stands on numbers of believers. Whenever the appeal is made – no matter how indirectly – to numbers, proclamation is then and
there made, that religion is not. He that finds God a sweet,
enveloping thought to him never counts his company.
When I sit in that presence, who shall dare to come in?

3

*Emerson makes the case for the virtue of holistic/
dynamic reasoning against the static/analytic approach, and as always, the poet is his model.*

Science was false by being unpoetical. It assumed to explain a reptile or mollusk, and isolated it, – which is hunting for life in graveyards. A reptile or mollusk or man or angel only exists in system, in relation. The metaphysician, the poet, only sees each animal form as an inevitable step in the path of the creating mind. The Indian, the hunter, the boy with his pets, have sweeter knowledge of these than the savant. We use semblances of logic until experience puts us in possession of real logic. The poet knows the missing link by the joy it gives. The poet gives us the eminent experiences only, – a god stepping from peak to peak, nor planting his foot but on a mountain.

 Emerson turns his attention to what we now describe as the advantages of "student-centered" teaching.

I advise teachers to cherish mother-wit. I assume that you will keep the grammar, reading, writing and arithmetic in order; 'tis easy and of course you will. But smuggle in a little contraband wit, fancy, imagination, thought. If you have a taste which you have suppressed because it is not shared by those about you, tell them that. Set this law up, whatever becomes of the rules of the school: they must not whisper, much less talk; but if one of the young people says a wise thing, greet it, and let all the children clap their hands. They shall have no book but school-books in the room; but if one has brought in a Plutarch or Shakespeare or Don Quixote or Goldsmith or any other good book, and understands what he reads, put them at once of the head of the class. Nobody shall be disorderly, or leave his desk without permission, but if a boy runs from his bench, or a girl, because the fire falls, or to check some injury that a little

dastard is inflicting behind his desk on some helpless sufferer, take away the medal from the head of the class and
give it on the instant to the brave rescuer.

5   *Emerson was not a fan of the whaling industry, as*
    we learn from a letter he wrote to Abby Adams, the
    ten-year-old adopted daughter of his Boston friend
    and financial adviser, Abel Adams.

Do you know where New Bedford lies on the map? It is
worth knowing, for though it is a small town it has more
ships than any other towns in the United States except
New York & Boston. At least they say so here. All these
vessels are employed in chasing the poor whale wherever
he swims all around the globe, that they may tear off his
warm jacket of blubber & melt it down into oil for your
lamp, & to steal from him his bone to make stays & para-
sols for ladies. If you get the volume of Harper's Family
Library called "Polar Seas & Regions" which is a very
interesting book you'll find a good account of this fishery.
Wait till I come home & I will lend it to you.

6   *Although he is, as always, thrilled to be in the New*
    Hampshire mountains, Emerson is not optimistic
    about New Hampshire people joining in the social
    reform he believed to be so sorely needed.

I see movement, I hear aspirations, but I see not how the
great God prepares to satisfy the heart in a new order of
things. No church no state will form itself to the eye of
desire & hope. Even when we have extricated ourselves
from all the embarrassment of the social problem it does
not please the oracle to emit any light on the *mode* of in-

dividual life. A thousand negatives it utters clear & strong on all sides, but the sacred affirmative it hides in the deepest abyss. We do not see that heroic resolutions will absolve men from those *tides* which a most fatal moon heaps & levels in the moral emotive & intellectual nature. . . . Perhaps there must be austere elections & determinations before any clear vision of the way is given. . . . I read somewhere that facts were the stuff of letters, but I lead the life of a blade of grass in mere wind & sun & have no other events than the weather.

7

All things are double, one against another, – Tit for tat; an eye for an eye; a tooth for a tooth; blood for blood; measure for measure; love for love. – Give and it shall be given you.

8

Emerson set sail from Liverpool to New York on Wednesday, September 4th, 1833, with thirteen other cabin passengers and sixteen persons in steerage. On the Sabbath, his thoughts turn to God, and his differences with the conventional religionists of his day. Today his revelations might sound familiar to students of Buddhism or Taoism.

It is the old revelation, that perfect beauty is perfect goodness, it is the development of the wonderful congruities of the moral law of human nature. Let me enumerate a few of the remarkable properties of that nature. A man contains all that is needful to his government within himself. He is made a law unto himself. All real good or evil that can befall him must be from himself. He is not to live to the future as described to him, but to live the real future by living to the real present. The highest revelation is that God is in every man.

9 *Emerson came to believe that he could not, in good conscience, continue to administer the ritual of communion. He was convinced that "most men find the bread and wine no aid to devotion ... to eat bread is one thing; to love the precepts of Christ is quite another," he said. In his sermon of September 9th, 1832, he made this position clear and offered to resign if the congregation did not agree with him. In October they accepted his resignation from the ministry.*

This mode of commemorating Christ is not suitable to me. That is reason enough why I should abandon it. If I believed it was enjoined by Jesus on his disciples, and that he even contemplated making permanent this mode of commemoration, every way agreeable to an Eastern mind, and yet on trial was disagreeable to my own feelings, I should not adopt it. I should choose other ways which, as more effectual upon me, he would approve more. For I choose that my remembrances of him should be pleasing, affecting, religious. I will love him as a glorified friend, after the free way of friendship, and not pay him a stiff sign of respect, as men do those whom they fear. A passage read from his discourses, a moving provocation to works like his, any act or meeting which tends to awaken a pure thought, a flow of love, an original design of virtue, I call a worthy, a true commemoration.

Emerson once wrote that "dreams acquaint us with what the day omits," and one might speculate that the dream he records here is trying to bring to light some unconscious conflicts about his career as a lecturer.

Last night a pictorial dream fit for Dante. I read a discourse somewhere to an assembly, & rallied in the course of it to find that I had nearly or quite fallen asleep. Then presently I went into what seemed a new house, the inside wall of which had many shelves led into the wall, on which great & costly Vases of Etruscan & other richly adorned pottery stood. The wall itself was unfinished, & I presently noticed great clefts, intended to be filled with mortar or brickwork, but not yet filled, & the wall which held all these costly vases, threatening to fall. Then I noticed in the centre shelf or alcove of the wall a man asleep, whom I understood to be the architect of the house. I called to my brother William who was near me, & pointed to this sleeper as the architect, when the man turned, & partly arose, & muttered something about a plot to expose him . . . what could I think of the purpose of Jove who sends the dream?

11

I think wealth has lost much of its value, if it have not wine. I abstain from wine only on account of the expense. When I heard that Mr. Sturgis had given up wine, I had the same regret that I had lately in hearing that Mr. Bowditch had broken his hip; a millionaire without wine, & a millionaire that must lie in bed.

12 *Emerson at twenty-five gives a hint of what will later be his sympathy with the Hindu notion of Maia, or illusion. Here it takes the form of an analysis of hubris.*

The true way to consider things is this: Truth says, Give yourself no manner of anxiety about events, about the consequences of actions. They are really of no importance to us. They have another Director, controller, guide. The whole object of the universe to us is the formation of character. If you think you came into being for the purpose of taking an important part in the administration of events, to guard a province of the moral creation from ruin, and that its salvation hangs on the success of your single arm, you have wholly mistaken your business.

13 *In his advocacy of Idealism, Emerson promoted the faculty of "Reason" as the power that might "tend to relax the despotism of the senses."*

When the eye of Reason opens, to outline and surface are at once added grace and expression. These proceed from imagination and affection, and abate somewhat all the angular distinctness of objects. If the Reason be stimulated to more earnest vision, outlines and surfaces become transparent, and are no longer seen: causes and spirits are seen through them. The best, the happiest moments of life, are these delicious awakenings of the higher powers, and the reverential withdrawing of nature before its God.

14 *Emerson, in his essay, "Manners," may be a little premature in his estimate of the state of women's*

rights, but he is quite clear that he hopes women
will lead the way if there is to be reform.

The open air and the fields, the street and public chambers
are the places where Man executes his will; let him yield or
divide the sceptre at the door of the house. Woman, with
her instinct of behavior, instantly detects in man a love of
trifles, any coldness or imbecility, or, in short, any want of
that large, flowing, and magnanimous deportment which is
indispensable in the hall. Our American institutions have
been friendly to her, and at this moment I esteem it a chief
felicity of this country, that it excels in women. A certain
awkward consciousness of inferiority in the men may give
rise to the new chivalry in behalf of Woman's Rights. Certainly let her be as much better placed in the laws and in
social forms as the most zealous perfect reformer can ask,
but I confide so entirely in her inspiring and musical nature,
that I believe only herself can show us how she shall be
served.

15

This belief that the higher use of the material world is to
furnish us types or pictures to express the thoughts of the
mind, is carried to its logical extreme by the Hindoos,
who, following Buddha, have made it the central doctrine
of their religion that what we call Nature, the external
world, has no real existence, – is only phenomenal. Youth,
age, property, condition, events, persons, – self, even, – are
successive *maias* (deceptions) through which Vishnu mocks
and instructs the soul. I think Hindoo books the best gym-
nastics for the mind, as showing treatment.

16 *Sa'di (Musleh, Al-Din, Shaikh), was one of Persia's greatest poets, and ultimately became Emerson's favorite, and, in 1842, the subject of his poem, "Saadi" (Emerson's spelling).*

SAADI

God, who gave to him the lyre
Of all mortals the desire,
For all breathing men's behoof,
Straitly charged him, "Sit aloof;"
Annexed a warning, poets say,
To the bright premium,–
Ever, when twain together play,
Shall the harp be dumb. . . .

Yet Saadi loved the race of men,–
No churl, immured in cave or den;
In bower and hall
He wants them all,
Nor can dispense
With Persia for his audience;
They must give ear,
Grow red with joy and white with fear;
But he has no companion;
Come ten, or come a million,
Good Saadi dwells alone.

17 *While returning from England in 1833, Emerson's shipboard conversations lead him to contemplate his definition of morals.*

Yesterday I was asked what I mean by morals. I replied that I cannot define, and care not to define. It is man's business to observe, and the definition of moral nature must be the slow result of years, of lives, of states, perhaps of being. Yet in the morning watch on my berth I thought that morals is the science of the laws of human action as respects right and wrong. Then I shall be asked, And what is Right? Right is a conformity to the laws of nature as far as they are known to the human mind.

18 *Once again Emerson extols astronomy, but he is not quite as enthusiastic about college students.*

Of all tools, an observatory is the most sublime. And these mountains give inestimable worth to Williamstown & Massachusetts. But for the mountains, I don't quite like the proximity of a college & its noisy students. To enjoy the hills as poet, I prefer simple farmers as neighbors....

What is so good in a college as an observatory? The sublime attaches to the door & to the first stair you ascend, that this is the road to the stars. Every fixture & instrument in the building, every nail & pin has a direct reference to the Milky-Way, the fixed stars, & the nebulae, & we leave Massachusetts & the Americas & history outside at the door, when we come in.

19

Introduce a base person among gentlemen; it is all to no purpose; he is not their fellow. Every society protects itself. The company is perfectly safe, and he is not one of them, though his body is in the room.

20 *Almost two hundred years after he first wrote these words, the climax of one of Emerson's most famous essays, "Self-Reliance", is still a resounding challenge.*

It is only as a man puts off all foreign support, and stands alone, that I see him to be strong and to prevail. He is weaker by every recruit to his banner. Is not a man better than a town? Ask nothing of men, and in the endless mutation, thou only firm column must presently appear the upholder of all that surrounds thee. He who knows that power is inborn, that he is weak because he has looked for good out of him and elsewhere, and so perceiving, throws himself unhesitatingly on his thought, instantly rights himself, stands in the erect position, commands his limbs, works miracles; just as a man who stands on his feet is stronger than a man who stands on his head.

So use all that is called Fortune. Most men gamble with her, and gain all, and lose all, as her wheel rolls. But do thou leave as unlawful these winnings, and deal with Cause and Effect, the chancellors of God. In the Will work and acquire, and thou hast chained the wheel of Chance, and shalt sit hereafter out of fear from her rotations. A political victory, a rise of rents, the recovery of your sick, or the return of your absent friend, or some other favorable event, raises your spirits, and you think good days are preparing for you. Do not believe it. Nothing can bring you peace but yourself. Nothing can bring you peace but the triumph of principles.

21 *Emerson, the constant reader, offers a subtle definition of what constitutes a literary "classic."*

The permanence of all books is fixed by no effort friendly or hostile, but by their own specific gravity, or the intrinsic importance of their contents to the constant mind of man.

 22 *For Emerson, the worship of nature was a personal experience almost daily, and directly involved the world around him in Concord, on his beloved Musketaquid River.*

It seems as if the day was not wholly profane, in which we have given heed to some natural object. The fall of snowflakes in a still air, preserving to each crystal its perfect form; the blowing of sleet over a wide sheet of water, and over plains, the waving rye-field, the mimic waving of acres of houstonia, whose innumerable florets whiten and ripple before the eye; the reflections of trees and flowers in glassy lakes; the musical steaming odorous south wind, which converts all trees to windharps; the crackling and spurting of hemlock in the flames; or of pine logs, which yield glory to the walls and faces in the sittingroom, – these are the music and pictures of the most ancient religion. My house stands in low land, with limited outlook, and on the skirt of the village. But I go with my friend to the shore of our little river, and with one stroke of the paddle, I leave the village politics and personalities, yes, and the world of villages and personalities behind, and pass into a delicate realm of sunset and moonlight, too bright almost for spotted man to enter without noviciate and probation.

23 *Preparing frantically for an examination that will license him to preach, Emerson falls prey to familiar psychosomatic symptoms.*

Health, action, happiness. How they ebb from me! Poor Sisyphus saw his stone stop once at least when Orpheus chaunted [*sic*]. I must roll mine up & up & up how high a hill. . . . It would give me very great pleasure to be well. It is mournful, the expectation of ceasing to be an object of hope, that we may become objects of compassion; and then go gloomily to *nothing* in the eye of the world before we have had one opportunity of turning to the sun what we know is our best side.

24 *Although he was born in Boston, Emerson, at fifty, is certainly no lover of the city.*

Rest on your humanity, and it will supply you with strength and hope and vision for the day. Solitude and the country, books, and openness, will feed you; but go to the city – I'm afraid there is no morning in Chestnut Street, it is full of rememberers, they shun each others' eyes, they are all wrinkled with memory of the tricks they have played, or mean to play, each other, of petty arts and aims all contracting and lowering their aspect and character.

25 *Among the modern phenomena that Emerson foresaw, one was his vision of our current love affair with second houses, gardening, and home décor.*

I think it will soon become the pride of this country to make gardens & adorn country houses. This is the fine art which especially fits us. Sculpture, painting, music, architecture do not arrive with us, but they seem as good as dead, & such life as they show is a sort of second childhood. But land we have in greater extent than ever did any people of the same power, and the new modes of travelling are making it easy to cultivate very distant tracts & yet remain in strict intercourse with the great centres of trade & population. And the whole force of all the arts goes to facilitate the decoration of lands & dwellings. A garden has this advantage, that it makes it indifferent where you live. If the landscape around you is pleasing, the garden shows it; if tame, it excludes it. A little grove which any farmer can find or cause to grow, will in a few years so fill the eye & mind of the inhabitant, as to make cataracts & chains of mountains quite unnecessary.

 Emerson's endorsement of the "occult arts" is genuine, but his observation of 1842 is still far from accepted by the majority of his countrymen in 2003.

How slowly, how slowly we learn that witchcraft and ghostcraft, palmistry and magic, and all the other so-called superstitions, which, with so much police, boastful skepticism, and scientific committees, we had finally dismissed to the moon as nonsense, are really no nonsense at all, but subtle and valid influences, always starting up, mowing, muttering in our path, and shading our day.

27

Censure and Praise. – I hate to be defended in a newspaper. As long as all that is said is said *against* me, I feel a certain sublime assurance of success, but as soon as honied words of praise are spoken for me, I feel as one that lies unprotected before his enemies.

28

*Is this a hint that Emerson realized his suscepti-
bility to the tuberculosis that was so common in his
family? Or recognition of what would come to be
known as his aloofness — a charge of which he was
aware, and which he both denied and admitted.*

I was born cold. My bodily habit is cold. I shiver in and
out; don't heat to the good purposes called enthusiasm a
quarter so quick and kindly as my neighbors.

29

*Probably no one has ever had a more balanced view
of the transitory nature of fame.*

Fame. I confess there is sometimes a caprice in fame, like
the unnecessary eternity given to these minute shells and
antediluvian fishes, leaves, ferns, yea, ripples and rain drops,
which have come safe down through a vast antiquity, with
all its shocks, upheavals, deluges, and volcanoes, wherein
everything noble in art and humanity had perished, yet
these snails, periwinkles, and worthless dead leaves come
staring and perfect into our daylight. — What is Fame, if
every snail or ripple or raindrop shares it?

30

The method of nature: who could ever analyze it? That
rushing stream will not stop to be observed. We can never
surprise nature in a corner; never find the end of a thread;
never tell where to set the first stone. The bird hastens to
lay her egg: the egg hastens to be a bird. The wholeness
we admire in the order of the world, is the result of
infinite distribution. Its smoothness is the smoothness of

the pitch of the cataract. Its permanence is a perpetual in-choation. Every natural fact is an emanation, and that from which it emanates is an emanation also, and from every emanation is a new emanation. If anything could stand still, it would be crushed and dissipated by the torrent it resisted, and if it were a mind, would be crazed; as insane persons are those who hold fast to one thought, and do not flow with the course of nature. Not the cause, but an ever novel effect, nature descends always from above. It is unbroken obedience.

·OCTOBER·

1

These halcyons may be looked for with a little more assurance in that pure October weather, which we distinguish by the name of the Indian summer.

2 *Emerson's poem, "Hamatreya," (see July 5) is concerned with the illusion of "owning" earthly property. It concludes with the following reply from the earth itself.*

EARTH-SONG

"Mine and yours;
Mine, not yours.
Earth endures;
Stars abide –
Shine down in the old sea;
Old are the shores;
But where are the old men?
I who have seen much
Such have I never seen.

"The lawyer's deed,"
Ran sure
In tail,
To them, and their heirs
Who shall succeed
Without fail
Forevermore.

"Here is the land
Shaggy with wood

With its old valley,
Mound and flood.
But the heritors?
Fled, like the flood's foam.
The lawyer, and the laws,
And the kingdom,
Clean swept herefrom.

They called me theirs
Who so controlled me
Yet every one
Wished to stay, and is gone
How am I theirs,
If they cannot hold me,
But I hold them?"

When I heard the earth-song
I was no longer brave;
My avarice cooled
Like lust in the chill of the grave.

3

Emerson is clearly content with what he sees as his vocation: being the painter of the possible.

People came, it seems, to model lectures with expectation that I was to realize the Republic I described, & ceased to come when they found this reality no nearer. They mistook me. I am & always was a painter. I paint still with might & main, & choose the best subjects I can. Many have I seen come & go with false hopes & fears, and dubiously affected by my pictures. But I paint on. I count this distinct vocation, which never leaves me in doubt what to do but in all times, places, & fortunes, gives me an open future, to be the great felicity of my lot.

4
Always considering two sides of every issue, and despite his anti-establishment disposition, Emerson contends that when it comes to the matter of Reform or Conservatism, "each is a good half, but a bad whole."

We are reformers in spring and summer; in autumn and winter, we stand by the old; reformers in the morning, conservers at night. Reform is affirmative, conservatism negative; conservatism goes for comfort, reform for truth. Conservatism is more candid to behold another's worth; reform more disposed to maintain and increase its own. Conservatism makes no poetry, breathes no prayer, has no invention; it is all memory. Reform has no gratitude, no prudence, no husbandry. It makes a great difference to your figure and to your thought, whether your foot is advancing or receding. Conservatism never puts the foot forward; in the hour when it does that, it is not establishment, but reform. Conservatism tends to universal seeming and treachery, believes in a negative fate; believes that men's temper governs them.

5

Converse with a mind that is grandly simple, and literature looks like word-catching. The simplest utterances are worthiest to be written, yet are they so cheap, and so things of course, that, in the infinite riches of the soul, it is like gathering a few pebbles off the ground, or bottling a little air in a phial, when the whole earth and the whole atmosphere are ours. Nothing can pass there, or make you one of the circle, but the casting aside your trappings, and dealing man to man in naked truth, plain confession, and omniscient affirmation.

6 *Fourteen years after their first meeting Emerson still finds Carlyle imposing.*

An immense talker, and, altogether, as extraordinary in that as in his writings; I think even more so. You will never discover his real vigor and range, or how much more he might do than he has ever done, without seeing him. My few hours discourse with him, long ago, in Scotland, gave me not enough knowledge of him; and I have now, at last, been taken by surprise by him.

He is not mainly a scholar like the most of my acquaintances, but a very practical Scotchman, such as you would find in any saddler's or iron-dealer's shop, and then only accidentally and by a surprising addition the admirable scholar and writer he is.

7 *Emerson offers a rare but clear definition of what he means by the soul.*

All goes to show that the soul in man is not an organ, but animates and exercises all the organs; is not a function, like the power of memory, of calculation, of comparison, but uses these as hands and feet; is not a faculty, but a light; is not the intellect or the will, but the master of the intellect and the will; is the background of our being, in which they lie, – an immensity not possessed and that cannot be possessed.

8 *Emerson answers one of his most vocal critics, Henry Ware, Jr., who was a spokesman for those in Cambridge and Boston who declared him a "heretic."*

I could not give account of myself, if challenged. I could not possibly give you one of the arguments you cruelly hint at, on which any doctrine of mine stands. For I do not know what arguments mean, in reference to any expression of thought. I delight in telling what I think; but, if you ask me how I dare say so, or, why it is so, I am the most helpless of mortal men. I do not even see that either of these questions admits of any answer. So that, in the present droll posture of my affairs, when I see myself suddenly raised into the importance of a heretic, I am very uneasy when I advert to the supposed duties of such a personage, who is to make good his thesis against all comers.

I certainly shall do no such thing. I shall read what you and other good men write, as I have always done, – glad when you speak my thoughts, and skipping the page that has nothing for me. I shall go on, just as before, seeing whatever I can, and telling what I see; and, I suppose, with the same fortune that has hitherto attended me.

9 *Emerson, in a pantheistic vein, reminds his friend Sarah Ann Clarke (a member of the Transcendental Club) that he believes divine thoughts to be found in the October woods of Concord.*

The sea, the firmament, the forest are the work of pure soul; in them therefore we can so easily pray & aspire; whilst we are so easily checked in the presence of man & his works, or Impure Soul. In these beautiful days which are now passing, go into the forest & the leaves hang silent & sympathetic, unobtrusive & related, like the thoughts which they so hospitably enshrine. Could they tell their sense, they would become the thoughts we have; could our thoughts take form they would hang as sunny leaves. And yet it is not by direct study of these enchantments that their sense is to be extorted, but by manlier & total methods, by doing & being. Conscience is the key to botany; by more life & not by microscopes must I learn the essence of a tree.

10 *Like all writers, Emerson has an idea of how he would like to be read, and he confides a vision of his ideal reader to his journal.*

I would have my book read as I have read my favorite books, not with explosion & astonishment, a marvel and a rocket, but a friendly & agreeable influence stealing like the scent of a flower or the sight of a new landscape on a traveller. I neither wish to be hated & defied by such as I startled, nor to be kissed and hugged by the young whose thoughts I stimulate.

11

As there is a science of stars, called astronomy; a science of quantities, called mathematics; a science of qualities, called chemistry; so is there is science of sciences – I call it the Dialectic – which is the Intellect discriminating the false and the true. It rests on the observation of identity and diversity; for to judge is to unite to an object the notion which belongs to it.

12 *After one of his intense conversations with Margaret Fuller, Emerson's tangled emotions emerge in this contemplative journal entry.*

I would that I could, and I know afar off that I cannot give the lights & shades, the hopes & outlooks that come to me in these strange, cold-warm, attractive-repelling conversations with Margaret, whom I always admire, most revere when I nearest see, and sometimes love, yet whom I freeze, & who freezes me to silence, when we seem to promise to come nearest. Yet perhaps my old motto holds true here also, *"And the more falls I get, move faster on."*

13

I much prefer the company of plough-boys and tin-pedlers, to the silken and perfumed amity which celebrates its days of encounter by a frivolous display, by rides in a curricle [a two-wheeled chaise drawn by two horses abreast] and dinners at the best taverns.

14 *On a sea voyage, the* Bhagavad Gita *(or Geeta as Emerson spelled it) was a valued companion in leisure hours.*

I owed – my friend & I owed – a magnificent day to the *Bhagavad Geeta*. It was the first of books; it was as if an empire spake to us, nothing small or unworthy but large, serene, consistent, the voice of an old intelligence which in another age & climate had pondered & thus disposed of the same questions which exercise us. Let us not now go back & apply a minute criticism to it, but cherish the venerable oracle.

15 *After forty-eight years of writing, Emerson records in his journal some clear ideas on how to do it well.*

Good Writing. All writing should be selection in order to drop every dead word. Why do you not save out of your speech or thinking only the vital things – the spirited mot which amused or warmed you when you spoke it – because of its luck & newness. I have just been reading, in this careful book of a most intelligent & learned man, a number of flat conventional words & sentences. If a man would learn to read his own manuscript severely – becoming really a third person, & search only for what interested him, he would blot to purpose – & how every page would gain! Then all the words will be sprightly, & every sentence a surprise.

16 *Written when he was twenty, this letter from Emerson to his favorite aunt, Mary Moody Emerson, is typical of the way he looked to her for counsel for a large part of his life despite his aunt's strict Calvinism and her somewhat cold and "penetrating directness."*

I ramble among doubts to which my reason offers no solution. Books are old & dull & unsatisfactory, the pen of a living witness & faithful lover of these mysteries of Providence is worth all the volumes of all the centuries. . . . What is the ordinary effect of an inexplicable enigma? Is it not to create opposition, ridicule, & bigoted skepticism? Does the Universe great & glorious in its operation aim at the slight of a mountebank who produces a wonder among the ignorant by concealing the causes of unexpected effects? . . . So please tell me what reply your active meditations have forged in metaphysical armoury to what is the Origin of Evil? And what becomes of the poor Slave born in chains living in stripes & toil for, who has never heard of virtue & never practiced it & dies cursing God & man? . . . Must he die in Eternal Darkness because it has been his lot to live in the Shadow of death?

17 *Even though in the summer of 1855 Emerson had written his letter to Walt Whitman "greeting him at the beginning of a great career," (see entry for July 21), barely ten months later he sent the book to his good friend Thomas Carlyle with an almost cynical suggestion. Carlyle did, indeed, find* Leaves of Grass *fit only to light fires.*

Dear Carlyle,

When I ceased to write to you for a long time I said to myself, – If anything really good should happen here, – any stroke of good sense or virtue in our politics, or of great sense in a book, – I will send it on to the formidable man; but I will not repeat to him every month, that there are no news. Thank me for my resolution, & for keeping it through the long night. One book, last summer came out in New York, a nondescript monster which yet has terrible eyes & buffalo strength & was indisputably American, – which I thought to send you; but the book throve so badly with the few to whom I showed it, & wanted good morals so much, that I never did. Yet I believe now again, I shall. It is called "Leaves of Grass," – was written & printed by a journeyman printer in Brooklyn, N. Y. named Walter Whitman, and after you have looked into it, if you think, as you may, that it is only an auctioneer's inventory of a warehouse you can light your pipe with it.

18 *Emerson's "spherules of force" appear to be precursors of what twentieth-century physicists discovered when they found that the atom was not stable and solid, but really a bundle of energy, moving at astonishing speed.*

First innuendoes, then broad hints, then smart taps are given, suggesting that nothing stands still in Nature but death; that the creation is on wheels, in transit, always passing into something else, streaming into something higher; that matter is not what it appears; – that chemistry can blow it all into gas. Faraday, the most exact of natural philosophers, taught that when we should arrive at the monads, or primordial elements (the supposed little cubes or prisms of which all matter was built up), we should not find cubes, or prisms, or atoms, at all, but spherules of force.

19

When the spirit is not master of the world, then it is its dupe. Yet the little man takes the great hoax so innocently, works in it so headlong and believing, is born red, and dies gray, arranging his toilet, attending on his own health, laying traps for sweet food and strong wine, setting his heart on a horse or a rifle, made happy with a little gossip or a little praise, that the great soul cannot choose but laugh at such earnest nonsense.

20   *After an editorial attack on him in the newspaper, Emerson takes a philosophical approach to criticism and once again tries to turn the experience into a lesson.*

A believer, a mind whose faith is consciousness, is never disturbed because other persons do not yet see the fact which he sees. It is plain that there are two classes in our educated community: first; Those who confine themselves to the facts in their consciousness; and secondly; Those who superadd sundry propositions. The aim of a true teacher now would be to bring men back to a trust in God & destroy before their eyes these idolatrous propositions: to teach the doctrine of the perpetual revelation.

21   *The major theme of "Self-Reliance" emerges again, ranking the inner man as far superior to any book.*

I am sure of this, that by going much alone a man will get more of a noble courage in thought and word than from all the wisdom that is in books.

22   *One can imagine that this note of admiration for total simplicity might have been a subject of conversation between Emerson and his dear friend Henry Thoreau.*

To find the unity in diversity is the role of the seeker of laws. When we find the unity behind the complex array of nature, we find the inherent simplicity of nature and are at home in it. We can never be at peace while we exist in a myriad of facts.

 Emerson could be whimsical, but even his "light" verse might contain a moral.

FABLE

The mountain and the squirrel
Had a quarrel;
And the former called the latter "Little Prig."
Bun replied,
"You are doubtless very big;
But all sorts of things and weather
Must be taken in together,
To make up a year
And a sphere.
And I think it no disgrace
To occupy my place.
If I'm not so large as you,
You are not so small as I
And not half so spry.
I'll not deny you make
A very pretty squirrel track;
Talents differ; all is well and wisely put;
If I cannot carry forests on my back,
Neither can you crack a nut."

24 *Emerson cannot quite bring himself to endorse some of the techniques that have, in our time, become part of "integrative medicine," but he does take the radical position of honoring them as the "loyal opposition."*

We obey the same intellectual integrity, when we study in exceptions the law of the world. Anomalous facts, as the never quite obsolete rumors of magic and demonology, and the new allegations of phrenologists and neurologists, are of ideal use. They are good indications. Homoeopathy is insignificant as an art of healing, but of great value as criticism on the hygeia or medical practice of the time. So with Mesmerism, Swedenborgism, Fourierism, and the Millennial Church; they are poor pretensions enough, but good criticism on the science, philosophy, and preaching of the day. For these abnormal insights of the adepts ought to be normal, and things of course.

25 *One wonders whether Emerson would be quite so enthusisatic about modern advertising as he appears here in this endorsement of "gay signs."*

Let the air in. The Advertising is one of the signs of our times; the hanging out a showy sign with the hitherto unheard of name of the huckster flourished in letters more gorgeous than ever the name of Pericles or of Jove was writ in. They do wisely who do thus. It is a petty title of nobility. The man is made one of the public in a small way. What he doth is of some importance; he is more responsible. His gay sign & far flying advertisement hold him at least to decency. So the publishing names of boys who have won school medals illustrates them, & bringing petty Broad street scuffle into court lets the air in, & purges blind alleys.

26

Superlatives in conversation have the effect of diminutives or negatives. "An exquisite delightful angel of a child," probably means a child not engaging.

 This spontaneous, poetic journal entry reflects the sense of liberation Emerson felt after his resignation from the ministry over the issue of administering the sacrament.

I will not live out of me.
I will not see with others eyes.
My good is good, my evil ill
I would be free – I cannot be
While I take things as others please to rate them.
I dare attempt to lay out my own road
That which myself delights in shall be Good
That which I do not want, – indifferent,
That which I hate is Bad. That's flat.
Henceforth, please God, forever I forgo
The yoke of men's opinions. I will be
Lighthearted as a bird & live with God.

 The idea of the twentieth-century thinker, Pierre Teilhard de Chardin, that consciousness is increasingly permeating the material world, is prefigured in Emerson's "Nature."

Nature is the incarnation of a thought, and turns to a thought again, as ice becomes water and gas. The world is mind precipitated, and the volatile essence is forever escaping again into the state of free thought. Hence the virtue and pungency of the influence on the mind, of natural objects, whether inorganic or organized. Man imprisoned, man crystallized, man vegetative, speaks to man impersonated. That power which does not respect quantity, which makes the whole and the particle its equal channel, delegates its smile to the morning, and distils its essence into every drop of rain. Every moment instructs, and every object: for wisdom is infused into every form. It has been poured into us as blood; it convulsed us as pain; it slid into us as pleasure; it enveloped us in dull, melancholy days, or in days of cheerful labor; we did not guess its essence, until after a long time.

 EROS

The sense of the world is short, –
Long and various the report, –
     To love and be beloved
Men and gods have not unlearned it;
And, how oft soe'er they've turned it,
     'Tis not to be improved.

30 *Once again Emerson finds reason to be optimistic, even as he delineates the age-old human dilemma of learning how to live simultaneously in the practical world and to participate in the Universal consciousness.*

We must be very suspicious of the deceptions of the element of time. It takes a good deal of time to eat or to sleep, or to earn a hundred dollars, and a very little time to entertain a hope and an insight which becomes the light of our life. We dress our garden, eat our dinners, discuss the household with our wives, and these things make no impression, are forgotten next week; but in the solitude to which every man is always returning, he has a sanity and revelations, which in his passage into new worlds he will carry with him. Never mind the ridicule, never mind the defeat: up again, old heart! – it seems to say, – there is victory yet for all justice; and the true romance which the world exists to realize, will be the transformation of genius into practical power.

31 *In his essay, "Demonology," Emerson extends his analysis of dreams to include other experiences with which we are all familiar.*

The name Demonology covers dreams, omens, coincidences, luck, sortilege, magic, and other experiences which shun rather than court inquiry, and deserve notice chiefly because every man has usually in a lifetime two or three hints in this kind which are specially impressive to him. They also shed light on our structure. The witchcraft of sleep divides with truth the empire of our lives.... 'Tis superfluous to think of the dreams of multitudes, the astonishment remains that one should dream; that we should resign so quietly this deifying Reason, and become the theatre of delirious shows, wherein time, space, persons, cities, animals, should dance before us in merry and mad confusion; a delicate creation outdoing the prime and flower of actual nature, antic comedy alternating with horrid pictures ... or we seem busied for hours and days in peregrinations over seas and lands, in earnest dialogues, strenuous actions for nothings and absurdities, cheated by spectral jokes and waking suddenly with ghastly laughter, to be rebuked by the cold, lonely, silent midnight, and to wake with confusion in memory among the gibbering nonsense to find the motive of this contemptible cacchination [*sic*].

·NOVEMBER·

1

A squirrel leaping from bough to bough, and making the wood but one wide tree for his pleasure, fills the eye not less than a lion – is beautiful, self-sufficing, and stands then and there for nature.

2 *Carlyle and Emerson helped promote each other's work in their respective countries. After giving report on book sales, Emerson here comments on the current state of the lecture business.*

I have nothing to tell you and no thoughts. I have promised a course of Lectures for this December, and am far from knowing what I am to say; this but the way to make sure of fighting into the new continent is to burn your ships. The "tender ears," as George Fox said of young men are always an effectual call to me ignorant to speak [*sic*]. I find myself so much more and freer on the platform of the lecture-room than in the pulpit, that I shall not much more use the last; and do now only in a little country chapel at the request of simple men to whom I sustain no other relation than that of preacher. But I preach in the Lecture-Room and then it tells, for there is no prescription. You may laugh, weep, reason, sing, sneer, or pray, according to your genius. It is the new pulpit and very much in vogue with my northern countrymen.

3 *In this passage from his lecture "New England Reformers," the direct and simple wisdom of Emerson is most evident.*

The life of man is the true romance, which when it is valiantly conducted will yield the imagination a higher joy than any fiction. All around us what powers are wrapped up under the coarse mattings of custom, and all wonder prevented. It is so wonderful to our neurologists that a man can see without his eyes, that it does not occur to them that it is just as wonderful that he should see with them; and that is ever the difference between the wise and the unwise; the latter wonders at what is unusual, the wise man wonders at the usual. Shall not the heart which has received so much, trust the Power by which it lives? May it not quit other leadings, and listen to the Soul that has guided it so gently and taught it so much, secure that the future will be worthy of the past?

4 *Throughout his life Emerson read and reread Shakespeare, whom he considered the greatest writer in the English language.*

Shakespeare fills us with wonder the first time we approach him. We go away, & work, & think, for years, & come again, he astonishes us anew. Then having drank deeply & saturated us with his genius, we lose sight of him for another period of years. By & by we return, & there he stands immeasurable as at first. We have grown wiser, but only that we should see him wiser than ever. He resembles a high mountain which the traveller sees in the morning & thinks he shall quickly near it & pass it & leave it behind. But he journeys all day till noon, till night. There still is the dim mountain close by him, having scarce altered its bearings since the morning light.

5 *Known always for friendliness and hospitality, Emerson confides to his journal that he can be driven to complete distraction by a guest – but can recover.*

I think four walls one of the best of our institutions. A man comes to me, & oppresses me by his presence: he looks very large and unanswerable. I cannot dispose of him whilst he stays, he quits the room, & passes not only out of the house, but as it were, out of the horizon; he is a mere phantasm or ghost. I think of him no more. I recover my sanity, the Universe dawns on me again.

6 *FATE*

That you are fair or wise is vain,
Or strong or rich or generous
You must have also the untaught strain
That sheds beauty on the rose.
There is a melody born of melody,
Which melts the world into the sea
Toil could never compass it;
Art its height could never hit;
It came never out of wit;
But a music music-born
Well may Jove and Juno scorn.
Thy beauty, if it lack the fire
Which drives me mad with sweet desire,
What boots it? What the soldier's mail,
Unless he conquer and prevail?
What all the goods thy pride which lift,
If thou pine for another's gift?

Alas! That one is born in blight,
Victim of perpetual slight:
When thou lookest on his face,
Thy heart saith, "Brother, go thy ways!
None shall ask thee what thou doest
Or care a rush for what thou knowest,
Or listen when thou repliest,
Or remember where thou liest,
Or how thy supper is sodden;"
And another is born
To make the sun forgotten
Surely he carries a talisman
Under his tongue;
Broad are his shoulders and strong
And his eye is scornful
Threatening, and young.
I hold it of little matter
Whether your jewel be of pure water,
A rose diamond or a white,
But whether it dazzle me with light.
I care not how you are dressed
In the coarsest or the best;
Nor whether your name is base or brave;
Nor for the fashion of your behavior;
But whether you charm me
Bid my bread feed and my fire warm me
And dress up Nature in your favor.
One thing is forever good;
That one thing is Success, —
Dear to the Eumenides,
And to all the heavenly brood.

Who bides at home, nor looks abroad,
Carries the eagles, and masters the sword.

7 *Emerson's reading of the great masters of English literature began early. By the time he was twenty-one he had developed some strong ideas about how to get the best from great writing.*

Let no man flatter himself with the hope of true good or solid enjoyment from the study of Shakespeare or Scott. Enjoy them as recreation. You cannot please yourself by going to stare at the moon; 'tis beautiful when in your *course* it comes.

8 *Although in his sixty-fifth year, and weakening, Emerson had been asked by William Forbes to conduct a private class for the "readings of poetry or prose, & conversation." He writes to James Thayer, accepting the proposition.*

To meet this request as nearly as I now can, I will say, that I fancy that, like every old scholar, I have points of rest & emphasis in literature. I know what books I have found unforgettable, & what passages in books. It will be most agreeable to me to indicate such. I should like, in poetry, especially, to mark certain authors & certain passages which I prize, & to state on what grounds I prize them; & to distinguish good poetry from what passes for good. I believe I might secure proper consideration for some remote & unfrequented sources. If the class would bear it, I have something to say on Oriental poetry, which poetry seems to me important, & yet not studied hitherto except as language, – for language as a part of paleontology. . . . Perhaps it will be found impossible to add ladies to the class, on account of the hours chosen. It will be equally agreeable to me to come in the afternoon or the evening. Only one condition is important to me, namely, that no person shall be coaxed to come.

 In his seventy-second year, and in one of the last entries in his journal, Emerson muses on the difficulty of understanding poetry.

The secret of poetry is never explained, – is always new. We have not got farther than mere wonder at the delicacy of the touch, and the eternity it inherits.

10 *Emerson's ambivalence about the priestly life reveals itself even in some of his poetry, and here extends to his theory of inspiration in a stanza that also contains the phrase he chose as his epitaph (see April 27th.)*

THE PROBLEM

I like a church, I like a cowl
I love a prophet of the soul;
And on my heart monastic isles
Fall like sweet strains, or pensive smiles;
Yet not for all his faith can see
Would I that cowled churchman be. . . .

*   *   *

These temples grew as grows the grass,
Art might obey, but not surpass

The passive Master lent his hand
To the vast soul that o'er him planned.
And the same power that reared the shrine
Bestrode the tribes that knelt within
Ever the fiery Pentecost
Girds with one flame the countless host,
Trances the heart through chanting choirs,
And through the priest the mind inspires.

11 *Emerson makes clear that in his day, "people-watching," let alone "people-ogling," was strictly forbidden by custom.*

How many attractions for us have our passing fellows in the streets both male & female, which our ethics forbid us to express which yet infuse us with so much pleasure into life. A lovely child, a handsome youth, a beautiful girl, a heroic man, a maternal woman, a venerable old man, charm us though strangers & we cannot say so, or even look at them but for a moment.

12 *These words, which Emerson wrote in 1837, make it clear why, in 1855, he will declare Walt Whitman's* Leaves of Grass *a masterpiece.*

The literature of the poor, the feelings of the child, the philosophy of the street, the meaning of household life, are the topics of the time. It is a great stride. It is a sign – is it not? – of vigor when the extremities are made active, when currents of warm life run into the hands and feet. I ask not for the great, the remote, the romantic; what is doing in Italy or Arabia; what is Greek art, or Provençal minstrelsy; I embrace the common, I explore and sit at the feet of the familiar, the low. Give me insight into to-day, and you may have the antique and future worlds. What would we really know the meaning of? The meal in the firkin; the milk in the pan, the ballad in the street; the use of the boat; the glance of the eye, the form and the gait of the body; show me the ultimate reason of these matters; show me the sublime presence of the highest spiritual cause lurking, as always it does lurk, in the suburbs and extremities of nature; let me see every trifle bristling with the polarity that ranges it instantly on an eternal law; and the shop, the plough, and the ledger referred to the like cause by which light undulates and poets sing, and the world lies no longer a dull miscellany and lumber-room, but has form and order; there is no trifle, there is no puzzle, but one design unites and animates the farthest pinnacle and the lowest trench.

13   *Emerson never tires of the world of what he calls "Nature," by which he obviously means to include all sensory material, animate and otherwise.*

How graceful & lively is a squirrel on a bough cracking a nut! How sylvan beautiful a stag bounding through Plymouth Woods! How like a smile of the earth is the first violet we meet in spring! Well, it was meant that I should see these & partake this agreeable emotion. Was it not? And was it not further designed that I should thereby be prompted to ask the relation of these natures to my own, & so the great word Comparative Anatomy has now leaped out of the womb of the Unconscious. I feel a cabinet in my mind unlocked by each of these new interests. Wherever I go, the related objects crowd on my Sense & I explore backward and wonder how the same things looked to me before my attention had been aroused.

14

A beautiful woman is a picture which drives all beholders nobly mad.

15

In this journal entry Emerson again states the case for humanism.

I could forgive your want of faith if you had any knowledge of the uttermost that man could be & do, if arithmetic could predict the last possibilities of instinct. But men are not made like boxes, a hundred, a thousand to order, & all exactly alike, of known dimension, & all their properties known; but no they come into nature through a nine months' astonishment & of a character each one incalculable & of extravagant possibilities; out of darkness & out of the Awful Cause they come to be caught up into this vision of a seeing, partaking, acting & suffering life, not foreknown, not forestimable but slowly or speedily they unfold new, unknown, mighty traits. Not boxes but these machines are alive, agitated, fearing, sorrowing.

16

Emerson puts into perspective the guilt we all feel over public and private inadequacies by urging us neither to deny nor be consumed by them.

When a zealot comes to me & represents the importance of the Temperance Reform my hands drop – I have no excuse – I honor him with shame at my own inaction.

Then a friend of the slave shows me the horrors of the Southern slavery – I cry guilty guilty! Then a philanthropist tells me the shameful neglect of the Schools by the Citizens. I feel guilty again.

Then I hear of Byron or Milton who drank soda water & ate a crust whilst others fed fat & I take the confessional anew. Then I hear that my friend has finished Aristophanes, Plato, Cicero & Grotius and I take shame to myself.

Then I hear of the generous Morton who offers a thousand dollars to the cause of Socialism, and I applaud & envy.

Then of a brave man who resists a wrong to the death and I sacrifice anew.

I cannot do all these things but these my shames are illustrious tokens that I have strict relations to them all. None of these causes are foreigners to me. My Universal Nature is thus marked. These accusations are part of me too. They are not for nothing.

17 *Sixteen years before the outbreak of the Civil War, Emerson takes a clear-cut position on the issue of civil rights for the "colored man" – and he does it right in his own New England region, in a letter to the Secretary of the New Bedford Lyceum.*

Dear Sir:

If I come to New Bedford, I should be ready to fix, say the first Tuesday of March, and the second. But I have to say, that I have indirectly received a report of some proceedings in your Lyceum, lately, which, by excluding others, I think ought to exclude me. My informant said, that the application of a colored person for membership by purchase of a ticket in the usual manner, had been rejected by a vote of the Lyceum; and this, for the first time. Now, as I think the Lyceum exists for popular education, as I work in it for that, and think it should bribe and importune the humblest and most ignorant to come in, and exclude nobody, or, if anybody, certainly the most cultivated, – this vote quite embarrasses me, and I should not know how to speak to the company. Besides, in its direct counteraction to the obvious duty and sentiment of New England, and of all freemen in regard to the colored people, the vote appears so unkind, and so unlooked for, that I could not come with any pleasure before the Society.

If I am misinformed, will you . . . have the goodness to send me the proceedings; or, if not printed, their purport; and oblige.

Yours respectfully,

18 *On November 18th, 1859, when Emerson made this speech in Boston, John Brown was under sentence of death, and was executed two weeks later. Brown had been a guest of Emerson at his home in Concord, and on the day Brown was executed Emerson made another address in Salem.*

It is the *reductio ad absurdum* of Slavery, when the governor of Virginia is forced to hang a man whom he declares to be a man of the most integrity, truthfulness and courage he has ever met. Is that the kind of man the gallows is built for? It were bold to affirm that there is within that broad Commonwealth, at this moment, another citizen as worthy to live, and as deserving of all public and private honor, as this poor prisoner.

But we are here to think of relief for the family of John Brown. To my eyes, that family looks very large and very needy of relief. It comprises his brave fellow sufferers in the Charlestown jail; the fugitives still hunted in the mountains of Virginia and Pennsylvania; the sympathizers with him in all the states; and I may say, almost every man who loves the Golden Rule and the Declaration of Independence, like him, and who sees what a tiger's thirst threatens him in the malignity of public sentiment in the slave states. It seems to me that a common feeling joins the people of Massachusetts with him.

19

'Tis the coldest November I have ever known. This morning the mercury is at 26. Yesterday afternoon cold fine ride with Ellery [Channing] to Sudbury Inn & mounted the side of Nobscot.... The landscape is democratic, not gathered into one city or baronial castle, but equally scattered into these white steeples, round which a town clusters in every place where six roads meet, or where a river branches or falls, or where the pan of soil is a little deeper. The horizon line marked by hills tossing like waves in a storm: firm indigo line. It is a pretty revolution which is effected in the landscape by simply turning your head upside-down, or, looking through your legs: an infinite softness & loveliness is added to the picture.... Or as Ellery declared it makes *Campagna* of it all at once; so he said, Massachusetts is Italy upside-down.

20 *Emerson casts a vote for the uses of skepticism, especially as it appears in the work of one of his heroes, the sixteenth-century essayist Montaigne.*

Skepticism is the attitude assumed by the student in relation to the particulars which society adores, but which he sees to be reverend only in their tendency and spirit. The ground occupied by the skeptic is the vestibule of the temple. Society does not like to have any breath of question blown on the existing order. But the interrogation of custom at all points is in an inevitable stage in the growth of every superior mind, and is the evidence of its perception of the flowing power which remains itself in all changes.

21

Every great and memorable community has consisted of formidable individuals, who, like the Roman or the Spartan, lent his own spirit to the state and made it great. Yet only by the supernatural is a man strong; nothing is so weak as an egotist. Nothing is mightier than we, when we are vehicles of a truth before which the state and the individual are alike ephemeral.

22 *Emerson makes specific the ways in which he sees the natural world, vegetable as well as animal, in a state of obvious evolution toward higher consciousness.*

Nature is always consistent, though she feigns to contravene her own laws. She keeps her laws and seems to transcend them. She arms and equips an animal to find its place and living in the earth, and at the same time she arms and equips another animal to destroy it. Space exists to divide creatures; but by clothing the sides of a bird with a few feathers she gives him a petty omnipresence. The direction is forever onward, but the artist still goes back for materials and begins again with the first elements on the most advanced stage; otherwise all goes to ruin. If we look at her work, we seem to catch a glance of a system in transition. Plants are the young of the world, vessels of health and vigor; but they grope ever upward towards consciousness; the trees are imperfect men, and seem to bemoan their imprisonment, rooted in the ground. The animal is the novice and probationer of a more advanced order.

23

Women see better than men. Men see easily if they do not expect to act. Women see quite without any wish to act. Men of genius are said to partake of the masculine & feminine traits. They have this feminine eye, a function so rich that it contents itself without asking any aid of the hand. Trifles may well be studied by him for he sees nothing insulated, the plaid of a cloak, the plaits of a ruffle, the wrinkles of a face absorb his attention & lead it to the root of these matters in Universal Laws.

24

And as the traveller who has lost his way throws his reins on his horse's back, and trusts to the instinct of the animal to find his road, so must we do with the divine animal who carries us through this world.

25 *Emerson sends a letter of thanks to Henry Wads-worth Longfellow, but delivers some strangely biased remarks about American Indians, particularly insensitive in view of his enlightened comments and social activism on behalf of black people.*

My dear Longfellow,

Sanborn brought me your good gift of Hiawatha, but I have not read it without many interruptions nor finished it till yesterday. I have always one foremost satisfaction in reading your books, that I am safe – I am in variously skillful hands but first of all they are safe hands. However, I find this Indian poem very wholesome, sweet & wholesome as maize very proper & pertinent to us to read, & showing a kind of manly sense of duty in the poet to write. The dangers of the Indians are, that they are really savage, have poor small sterile heads, – no thoughts, & you must deal very roundly with them, & find them in brains; and I blamed your tenderness now & then, as I read, in accepting a legend or a song, when they had so little to give. I should hold you to your creative function on such occasions. But the costume & machinery, on the whole, is sweet & melancholy, & agrees with the American landscape.

26

What is the hardest task in the world? To think. I would put myself where I have so often been in the attitude of meeting as it were face to face an abstract truth – & I cannot; I blench; I withdraw on this side, on that. I seem to know what he meant who said, "No man can see God face to face & live."

27

The fate of the poor shepherd, who, blinded and lost in the snow-storm, perishes in a drift within a few feet of his cottage door, is an emblem of the state of man. On the brink of the waters of life and truth, we are miserably dying.

28

Some years after Thoreau's death, Emerson finds what so many ensuing readers have discovered: Thoreau was not only a radical thinker but a powerful and original writer.

In reading Henry Thoreau's journal I am very sensible of the vigor of his constitution. That oaken strength that I noted when we walked or worked or surveyed wood lots, the same unhesitating hand with which a field-laborer accosts a piece of work which I should shun as a waste of strength, Henry shows in his literary task. He has muscle, & ventures on & performs feats which I am forced to decline. In reading him, I find the same thought, the same spirit that is in me, but he takes a step beyond & illustrates by excellent images that which I should have conveyed by a sleepy generality. 'Tis as if I went into a gymnasium, & saw youths leap, climb & swing with a force unapproachable – though their feats are only continuations of my initial grapplings and jumps.

29

"Fire," Aunt Mary said, "was a great deal of company;" & so is there company, I find, in Water. It animates the solitude. Then somewhat nearer to human society is in the hermit birds that harbor in the wood. I can do well for weeks with no other society than the partridge & the jay, my daily company.

30 *Emerson reminisces about his childhood and notes the changes Time has wrought.*

I was a little chubby boy trundling a hoop in Chauncey Place and spouting poetry from Scott & Campbell at the Latin School. But Time the little grey man has taken out of his vest pocket a great awkward house (in a corner of which I sit & write of him) some acres of land, several fullgrown & several very young persons, & seated them close beside me; then he has taken that chubbiness & that hoop quite away (to be sure he has left the declamation & the poetry) and here left a long lean person threatening soon to be a little grey man, like himself.

· DECEMBER ·

1

The whited air
Hides hills and woods, the river and the heaven,
And veils the farm-house at the garden's end.
The sled and travellers stopped, the courier's feet
Delayed, all friends shut out, the housemates sit
Around the radiant fire-place enclosed
In a tumultuous privacy of storm.

2

*In his "Lecture on the Times," read at Boston's
Masonic Temple, Emerson makes clear that abstractions like "history," "the Age," "the Times," are not
as significant as we suppose. "We talk of the world,
but we mean a few men and women."*

What is the reason to be given for this extreme attraction
which persons have for us, but that they are the Age? they
are the results of the Past; they are the heralds of the
Future. They indicate – these witty, suffering, blushing,
intimidating figures of the only race in which there are
individuals or changes, how far on the Fate has gone, and
what it drives at. As trees make scenery, and constitute the
hospitality of the landscape, so persons are the world to
persons. . . . Thoughts walk and speak, and look with eyes
at me, and transport me into new and magnificent scenes.
These are the pungent instructors who thrill the heart of
each of us, and makes all other teaching formal and cold.

3

*Emerson displays a keen understanding of the need
for exploring the psychology of teen-age children.*

The age of puberty is a crisis in the life of the man worth studying. It is the passage from the Unconscious to the Conscious; from the sleep of the Passions to their rage; from careless receiving to cunning providing; from beauty to use; from omnivorous curiosity to anxious stewardship; from faith to doubt; from maternal Reason to hard short-sighted Understanding; from Unity to disunion.

 Emerson reaffirms that he will not be bound by any of the labeled sects of religious practice but will continue the search for truth, wherever it may take him.

Do you imagine that because I do not say Luther's creed all his works are an offence to me? Far otherwise. I can animate them all that they shall live to me. I can worship in that temple as well as in any other. I have only to translate a few of the leading phrases into their equivalent verities, to adjust his almanack to my meridian & all the conclusions, all the predictions shall be strictly true. Such is the everlasting advantage of truth. Let a man work after a pattern he really sees & every man shall be able to find a correspondence between these works & his own & to turn them to some account in Rome, London, or Japan, from the first to the hundredth century.

5 *At the height of his own most productive literary decade, Emerson rallies his fellow New Englanders to offer their support to a new journal to be called* The Massachusetts Quarterly Review.

One would say there is nothing colossal in this country but its geography and its material activities; that the moral and intellectual effects are not on the same scale with the trade and production. There is no speech heard but that of auctioneers, newsboys, and the caucus. Where is the great breath of the New World, the voice of aboriginal nations opening new eras with hymns of lofty cheer? Our books and fine arts are imitation; there is a fatal incuriosity and disinclination in our educated men to new studies, critical talent, good professors, good commentators, but a lack of male energy. What more serious calamity can befall a people than a constitutional dulness and limitation?

The moral influence of the intellect is wanting. We hearken in vain for any profound voice speaking to the American heart, cheering timid good men, animating the youth, consoling the defeated, and intelligently announcing duties which clothe life with joy, and endear the face of land and sea to men.

6

What is it that interests us in biography? Is there not always a silent comparison between the intellectual & moral endowments portrayed & those of which we are conscious? The reason why the Luther, the Newton, the Bonaparte concerning whom we read, was made the subject of panegyric, is, that in the writer's opinion, in some one respect this particular man represented the idea of Man. As far as we accord with his judgment, we take the picture for a standard Man and so let every line accuse or approve our own ways of thinking & living by comparison.

7   *By Emerson's standards, the truly aristocratic man is completely nonviolent.*

Natural Aristocracy. It is a vulgar error to suppose that a gentleman must be ready to fight. The utmost that can be demanded of the gentleman is that he be incapable of a lie. There is a man who has good sense, is well-informed, well read, obliging, cultivated, capable, and has an absolute devotion to truth. He always means what he says, and says what he means, however courteously. You may spit upon him – nothing could induce him to spit upon you, – no praises, and no possessions, no compulsion of public opinion. You may kick him; – he will think it the kick of a brute: but he is not a brute, and will not kick you in return. But neither your knife and pistol, nor your gifts and courting will ever make the smallest impression on his vote or word; for he is truth's man, and will speak and act the truth until he dies.

8   *In his essay, "Circles," Emerson again echoes the Buddhist and Taoist precepts, which always urge us to disidentify ourselves from "events."*

The difference between talents and character is adroitness to keep the old and trodden round, and power and courage to make a new road to new and better goals. Character makes an overpowering present; a cheerful, determined hour, which fortifies all the company, by making them see that much is possible and excellent that was not thought of. Character dulls the impression of particular events. When we see the conqueror, we do not think much of any one battle or success. We see that we had exaggerated the difficulty. It was easy to him. The great man is not convulsible or tormentable; events pass over him without much impression. People say sometimes, 'See what I have overcome; see how cheerful I am; see how completely I have triumphed over these black events.' Not if they still remind me of the black event. True conquest is the causing the calamity to fade and disappear, as an early cloud of insignificant result in a history so large and advancing.

9

Yesterday, English visitors, and I waited all day when they should go. If we could establish the rule that each man was a guest in his own house, and when we had shown our visitors the passages of the house, the way to fire, to bread, and water, and thus made them as much at home as the inhabitant, did then leave them to the accidents of intercourse, and went about our ordinary business, – a guest would no longer be formidable.

10

Emerson waxed patriotic on a number of occasions, yet confesses a certain cynicism about patriotism too loudly proclaimed.

I confess I am a little cynical on some topics, and when a whole nation is roaring Patriotism at the top of its voice, I am fain to explore the cleanness of its hands and purity of its heart. I have generally found the gravest and most useful citizens are not the easiest provoked to swell the noise, though they may be punctual at the polls.

11

There is great delight in learning a new language. When the day comes in the scholar's progress unawares when he reads pages without recurrence to his dictionary, he shuts up his book with that sort of fearful delight with which the bridegroom sits down in his own house with the bride, saying, "I shall now live with you always."

12

In one of his final poems, "Terminus," Emerson seems to be reminding us that what he calls "force" and "genius" arise only if we make the choices and the effort to be vigorously awake, self-conscious in the creative sense.

Curse, if thou wilt, thy sires,
Bad husbands of their fires,
Who, when they gave thee breath,
Failed to bequeath
The needful sinew stark as once,
The Baresark marrow to thy bones,
But left a legacy of ebbing veins,
Inconstant heat and nerveless reins,–
Amid the muses left thee deaf and dumb,
Amid the gladiators, halt and numb.

13

Emerson's advice in his essay, "Experience," is undoubtedly meant to caution us against trying too hard to achieve spiritual revelation, or, for that matter, trying too hard to gain experience itself.

I prefer to say with the old prophet, "Seekest thou great things? Seek them not." Life is a boundless privilege, and when you pay for your ticket and get into the car [on the train] you have no guess what good company you shall find there. You buy much that is not rendered in the bill. Men achieve a certain greatness unawares, when working to another aim.... Nature does not like to be observed, and likes that we should be her fools and playmates. We may have the sphere [Earth] for our cricket-ball, but not a berry for our philosophy. Direct strokes she never gave us the power to make; all our blows glance, all our hits are accidents.

 As in the previous entry, Emerson is once again alerting us to the richness of accident and surprise.

The most attractive class of people are those who are powerful obliquely, and not by the direct stroke: men of genius, but not yet accredited; one gets the cheer of their light without paying too great a tax.

15 *Emerson had been approached by George Ripley, the moving force behind the prospective Brook Farm Community, to buy shares in the enterprise, and then, in a letter, Ripley had written Emerson urging him to join the community with his family. Sympathetic as he was to the idea of communal living, especially when it featured a mixture of intellectual and manual labor, he declines – but still feels guilty about the decision.*

My dear Sir,

It is quite time I made an answer to your proposition that I should join you in your new enterprise. The design appears to be so noble & humane, proceeding, as I plainly see, from a manly & expanding heart & mind that it makes me & all men its friends & debtors. It becomes a matter of conscience to entertain it friendly & to examine what it has for us. . . . I have decided not to join it & yet very slowly & I may almost say penitentially. . . . The ground of my decision is almost purely personal to myself. . . . That which determines me is the conviction that the Community is not good for me. Whilst I see it may hold out many inducements for others it has little to offer me which with resolution I cannot procure for myself. It seems to me that it would not be worth my while to make the difficult exchange of my property in Concord for a share in the new Household. . . . Here I have builded & planted: & here I have greater facilities to prosecute such practical enterprises as I may cherish, than I could probably find by any removal.

16 *In one way Emerson takes the responsibility for the mishandling of his lectures in the newspapers, but in December 1864, he still petitions his friend, James Thayer, to use influence to prevent reprinting of his texts. (Thayer, by the way, will accompany Emerson on his western trip seven years after this letter was written.)*

My dear Mr. Thayer,

If you have the ear of the "Daily Advertiser," & can without inconvenience, I wish you would ask the Editor to omit any report of my Lectures. The fault of the reports is doubtless owing to the lecture itself which lacks any method, or any that is easily apprehensible, but it distresses me a little to read them & more that others should. Of course to any general notice I have no objection but much to the rendering of sentences. And I should take it as a great kindness if it were omitted. But it is not worth giving you any trouble. Mr. Slack I believe made some such request & told me it was all settled but it is not all ended.

17 *It is not surprising that the man who so enjoyed the company of his lively circle of intellectual friends should make such an eloquent case for the benefits of conversation.*

Conversation, when it is best, is a series of intoxications. Not Aristotle, not Kant or Hegel, but conversation, is the right metaphysical professor. This is the true school of philosophy, − this the college where you learn what thoughts are, what powers lurk in those fugitive gleams, and what becomes of them; how they make history. A wise man goes to this game to play upon others, and to be played upon, and at least as curious to know what can be drawn from himself as what can be drawn from them. For, in discourse with a friend, our thought, hitherto wrapped in our consciousness, detaches itself, and allows itself to be seen as a thought, in a manner as new and entertaining to us as to our companions. For provocation of thought, we use ourselves and use each other. Some perceptions − I think the best − are granted to the single soul; they come from the depth, and go to the depth, and are the permanent and controlling ones. Others it takes two to find. We must be warmed by the fire of sympathy to be brought into the right conditions and angles of vision.

18 *Perhaps we hear in Emerson the inspiration for the modern slogan, "Be here now."*

We cannot overstate our debt to the Past, but the moment has the supreme claim. The Past is for us; but the sole terms on which it can become ours is its subordination to the Present. Only an inventor knows how to borrow, and every man is or should be an inventor. We must not tamper with the organic motion of the soul. 'Tis certain that thought has its own proper motion, and the hints which flash from it, the words overheard at unawares by the free mind, are trustworthy and fertile when obeyed and not perverted to low and selfish account. This vast memory is only raw material. The divine gift is ever the instant life, which receives and uses and creates, and can well bury the old in the omnipotency with which Nature decomposes all her harvest for recomposition.

19 *Emerson felt that every person has some sense of his or her own fate, destiny, calling, mission, or vocation. He sensed his while still in his twenties, and made this record of it.*

I read my commission in every cipher of nature, and know that I was made for another office, a professor of the Joyous Science, a detector and delineator of occult harmonies and unpublished beauties, a herald of civility, nobility, learning and wisdom; an affirmer of the One Law yet as one who should affirm it in music and dancing.

20 *Emerson sees the struggle between "reform" and "conservatism" as an eternal fact. Moreover, he sees it as a metaphor for the duality existing within individuals as well.*

It may be safely affirmed of these two metaphysical antagonists, that each is a good half, but an impossible whole. Each exposes the abuses of the other, but in a true society, in a true man both must combine. Nature does not give the crown of its approbation, namely beauty, to any action or emblem or actor but to one which combines both these elements; not to the rock which resists the waves from age to age, nor to the wave which lashes incessantly the rock, but this superior beauty is with the oak which stands with its hundred arms against the storms of a century, and grows every year like a sapling; or the river which ever flowing, yet is found in the same bed from age to age; or, greatest of all, the man who has subsisted for years amid the changes of nature, yet has distanced himself, so that when you remember what he was, and see what he is, you say "What strides! What a disparity is here!"

21 *The man who was sometimes mocked for his optimism could also fall prey to melancholy. But on this day, in 1823, he moves to defiance and identifies his existence with that of his soul.*

I say to the Universe, mighty one! thou art not my mother; Return to chaos if thou wilt; I shall still exist. If I owe my being it is to a destiny greater than thine. Star by star, world by world, system by system shall be crushed, – but I shall live.

22 *Emerson had resigned his pulpit in September 1832. A spell of ill health right after that prevented him from appearing again before the congregation, so on December 22nd he sent this letter to the Second Church and Society.*

I am no longer your minister, but am not the less engaged, I hope, to the love and service of the same external cause, the advancement, namely, of the kingdom of God in the hearts of men.... I rejoice to believe, that my ceasing to exercise the pastoral office among you, does not make any real change in our spiritual relation to each other. Whatever is most desirable and excellent therein, remains to us for, truly speaking, whoever provokes me to a good act or thought, has given me a pledge of his fidelity to virtue, – he has come under bonds to adhere to that cause to which we are jointly attached. And so I say to you, who have been my counsellors and co-operators in our Christian walk, that I am wont to see in your faces, the seals and certificates of our mutual obligations....

And now, brethren and friends, having return into your hands the trust you have honored me with – the charge of public and private instruction in this religious society, I pray God, that whatever seed of truth and virtue we have sown and watered together, may bear fruit unto eternal life.... In this faith and hope, I bid you farewell.

23 *Not in the least daunted by the uproar he had created in his Divinity School Address, Emerson went on to speak at other colleges. His address on "Literary Ethics" to the students of Dartmouth College*

again pointed out that the "scholar" had special
obligations to realize his own potential divinity.

The man who stands on the seashore, or who rambles in
the woods, seems to be the first man that ever stood on the
shore, or entered a grove, his sensations in the world are so
novel and strange. Whilst I read the poets, I think that nothing new can be said about morning and evening. But when
I see the daybreak, I am not reminded of these Homeric,
or Shakespearean, or Miltonic, or Chaucerian pictures. No;
but I feel perhaps the pain of an alien world; or world not
yet subdued by the thought; or I am cheered by the moist,
warm, glittering, budding, melodious hour, that takes down
the narrow walls of my soul, and extends its life and pulsa-
tion to the very horizon.... There is no event but sprang
somewhere from the soul of man; and therefore there is
none but the soul of man can interpret.... The whole
value of history, of biography, is to increase my self-trust,
by demonstrating what man can be and do.

24 *Emerson has another experience that reinforces his*
notion that we had all best expand on our unique
strengths.

Is it not true that every man has before him in his mind
room in one direction to which there is no bound, but in
every other direction he runs against a wall in a short
time? One course of thought, affection, action is for him
– that is his use, as the new men say. Let me embark in
political economy, in repartee, in fiction, in verse, in practical counsels ... and I am soon run aground; but let my
bark head its own way toward the law of laws, toward the

compensation or action and reaction of the moral universe and I sweep serenely over God's depths in an infinite sea.

25

At the performing of Handel's *Messiah* I heard some delicious strains & understood a very little of all that was told me. My ear received but little thereof. But as the master overpowered the littleness & incapableness of the performers, & made them conductors of his electricity, so it was easy to see what efforts nature was making through so many hoarse, wooden & imperfect persons to produce beautiful voices, fluid & soulguided men & women. The genius of nature could well be discerned. By right & might we should become participants of her invention, & not wait for morning & evening to know their peace, but prepossess it. I walked in the bright paths of sound, and liked it best when the long continuance of a chorus had made the ear insensible to the music, made it as if there was none, then I was quite solitary & at ease in the melodious uproar. Once or twice in the solos, when well sung, I could play tricks, as I like to do, with my eyes, darken the whole house & brighten & transfigure the central singer, and enjoy the enchantment.

 As he has in so many other contexts, Emerson sees, and reminds himself, that the miraculous and the mysterious lie in the mundane world.

"Miracles have ceased." Have they indeed? When? They had not ceased this afternoon when I walked into the wood and got into bright, miraculous sunshine, in shelter from the roaring wind. Who sees a pine-cone, or the turpentine exuding from the tree, or a leaf, the unit of vegetation, fall from its bough, as if it said, "the year is finished," or hears in the quiet, piny glen the chickadee chirping his cheerful note, or walks along the lofty, promontory-like ridges which, like natural causeways, traverse the morass, or gazes upward at the rushing clouds, or downward at a moss or a stone and says to himself, "Miracles have ceased"?

27 *As he approached his twentieth birthday, Emerson's mood alternated between existential angst and spiritual exhilaration. His verses at the time reflect his increasing philosophical Idealism.*

I am not poor, but I am proud
Of one inalienable right
Above the envy of the crowd –
Thought's holy light.

Better it is than gems or gold
And oh it cannot die,
But thought will glow when the Sun grows cold
And mix with Deity.

28 *Here we see Emerson prefiguring the essence of holistic theory: the fundamental drive in nature is the evolution of organisms into higher and higher forms.*

All the facts of the animal economy, sex, nutriment, gestation, birth, growth, are symbols of the passage of the world into the soul of man, to suffer there a change and reappear a new and higher form. This is true science. The poet alone knows astronomy, chemistry, vegetation and animation, for he does not stop at these facts, but employs them as signs. He knows why the plain or meadow of space was strown with these flowers we call suns and moons and stars; why the great deep is adorned with animals, with men, and gods, for in every word he speaks he rides on them as the horses of thought.

 Despite his optimism that the higher aspects of human nature would inevitably emerge, Emerson remained keenly aware of the contrast between the elements in the "double-consciousness." He addressed this in a lecture called "Success," which he delivered in Hartford in December 1858.

We live on different planes or platforms. There is an external life, which is educated at school, taught to read, write, cipher and trade; taught to grasp all the boy can get, urging him to put himself forward, to make himself useful and agreeable in the world, to write, run, argue and contend, unfold his talents, shine, conquer and possess.

But the inner life sits at home, and does not learn to do things, nor value these feats at all. 'Tis a quiet, wise perception. It loves truth because it is itself real; it loves right, it knows nothing else; but it makes no progress; was as wise in our first memory of it as now; is just the same now in maturity and hereafter in age, as it was in youth. We have grown to manhood and womanhood; we have powers, connection, children, reputations, professions: this makes no account of them all. It lives in the great present; it makes the present great. This tranquil, well-founded, wide-seeing soul is no express-rider, no attorney, no magistrate: it lies in the sun and broods on the world.

30   *Emerson offers some guidelines on contemplating immortality (reincarnation?).*

A man of thought is willing to die, willing to live; I suppose, because he has seen the thread on which the beads are strung, and perceived that it reaches up and down, existing quite independently of the present illusions. A man of affairs is afraid to die, is pestered with terrors, because he has not this vision, and is the victim of those who have moulded the religious doctrines into some neat and plausible system, as Calvinism, Romanism, or Swedenborgism, for household use. It is the fear of the young bird to trust its wings. The experiences of the soul fast outgrow this alarm. The saying of Marcus Antoninus it were hard to mend: "It were well to die if there be gods, and sad to live if there be none." I think all sound minds rest on a certain preliminary conviction, namely, that if it be best that conscious personal life shall continue, it will continue; if not best that it will not; and we, if we saw the whole, should of course see that it was better so.

31   *To Emerson, the end of the year is merely another day in the infinity of Time.*

There are no finalities in Nature. Everything is streaming. The Toricellian tube was thought to have made a vacuum; but no; over the mercury is the vapor of mercury. And the mysterious ether too enters as readily through the pores of glass as through fissures of a volcano.

If I come to stoppages, it is I that am wanting. To the wise navigator, beyond even the polar ice, is the Polynia, or open water, – a vast expanse.

ADDITIONAL READING

The original works of Ralph Waldo Emerson are generally available at libraries and bookshops. However, there are superb secondary sources, books that distill one or more aspects of his work and contain valuable commentaries and/or analyses. And there are several biographies or scholarly studies of the man and his work and times. Here is a selection of those titles I have found especially valuable:

Allen, Gay, *Waldo Emerson*, New York, Viking Press, 1981.

Atkinson, Brooks, ed., *The Complete Essays and Other Writings of Ralph Waldo Emerson*, New York, Modern Library, 1950.

Bode, Carl (in collaboration with Malcolm Cowley), eds., *The Portable Emerson*, New York, Penguin, 1981.

Cabot, James Elliott. *A Memoir of Ralph Waldo Emerson*, 2 vol., London, Houghton Mifflin, 1887.

Geldard., Richard, *The Spiritual Teachings of Ralph Waldo Emerson*, Great Barrington, Massachusetts, Lindisfarne Books, 2001.

Mumford, Lewis, ed., *Ralph Waldo Emerson: Essays and Journals*, Garden City, New York, International Collectors Library, 1968.

Myerson, Joel, ed., *The Selected Letters of Ralph Waldo Emerson*, New York, Columbia University Press, 1997.

Perry, Bliss, ed., *The Heart of Emerson's Journals*, New York, Dover Publications, 1995.

Porte, Joel, ed., *Emerson in His Journals*, Cambridge, The Belknap Press of Harvard University Press, 1982.

Richardson, Robert, *Emerson: The Mind on Fire*, Berkeley, California, University of California Press, 1995.

In addition to these books, there is a most unusual twenty-first century resource in the form of a web site called www.rwe.org *owned and maintained by Jim Manley, which contains an astonishing amount of Emerson material, and is linked to a number of other interesting sites relevant to the readers of Emerson.*

Finally, for those who wish to keep abreast of Emerson scholarship devoted to the study and appreciation of Emerson's life, writing, and legacy, the bulletin of The Emerson Society is an invaluable publication. Membership in the society is not limited to scholars or academics. Address inquiries to Robert D. Habich, Secretary/Treasurer, The Ralph Waldo Emerson Society, Department of English, Ball State University, Muncie, Indiana 47306-0460.

ACKNOWLEDGMENTS

I AM GRATEFUL to the entire staff of David R. Godine, Publisher, for their work. David, whom I have known and respected for more than thirty-five years, gave much of his vaunted talent and judgment to the publishing process. My editor, Elsbeth Lindner, gave Emerson and me her focused attention, and her suggestions and comments helped me to come closer to my original vision for the book. Carl W. Scarbrough is largely responsible for the handsome design and was gracious in letting me have some say about it. I am honored that Barry Moser, a preeminent artist much beloved by book people, consented to create the wonderful engravings that grace these pages. My association with all the talented people engaged by David Godine has been a pleasure.

The rightness of that association was intuited and arranged by Jill Kneerim. This is one more of the acts of kinship and loyalty Jill has done for me, and I am grateful that she is in my life.

We who make books are forever thanking people for "support," "encouragement," and "help." The words can describe hundreds of things, ranging from a letter of encouragement to a suggestion about syntax, from the loan of a reference book to the careful copy-editing of a whole chapter – a remarkable assortment of gestures without which writers and editors would be complete isolates. For such contributions, I thank the following, and though the conventions of listing them may appear to reduce their names to an alphabetical directory, that does not for a moment diminish my gratitude to every one of them: Margaret Bancroft, Barbara Smith Coleman, Web Coleman, Joan Grossman, Connell McGrath, Janet Malcolm, Mary Matyas, Barbara Mongan and the guides at the Ralph Waldo Emerson House, Bill Nagle, Nancy Nagle, Ron Ragusa, Lucy Rochambeau, Shanti Norris and the Smith Farm team, Lawrence Volper, and Leslie Perrin Wilson of the Concord Free Public Library.

For not only tolerating but welcoming my near-obsessive interest in Emerson and for her sensitive reviewing of every line of this book, I thank my wife, Ann Arensberg.

ABOUT THE EDITOR

RICHARD GROSSMAN spent many years as a book editor and publisher, first as vice-president of Simon & Schuster, and later as founder and president of Grossman Publishers. Since 1974 he has worked as a medical educator at Montefiore Medical Center and Beth Israel Medical Center in New York City and has been in practice as a psychotherapist in New York and Connecticut. He was contributing editor and columnist at *Health* magazine for nine years, and his writing has appeared in dozens of medical journals and popular magazines. His previous books include *Bold Voices, Choosing & Changing*, and *The Other Medicines*.

For more than forty years, Mr. Grossman has been a devoted student of Ralph Waldo Emerson, reading almost daily in the over fifty volumes of Emerson's writing and lectures. *A Year with Emerson* grew out of that involvement, and is published as a celebration of the 200th anniversary of Emerson's birth, May 25, 1803.

Richard Grossman lives in Salisbury, Connecticut.

A YEAR WITH EMERSON

has been set in a digital version of Monotype Bell, a face based
on the types Richard Austin cut in 1788 for John Bell's British
Type Foundry. Intended for an unrealized edition of the Book
of Common Prayer, the types enjoyed their first significant
success in Bell's daily newspaper, The Oracle. ❡ Although
Stanley Morison classed Bell as a modern face, Alexander
Lawson's description is perhaps more accurate: "a more faithful rendition of the transitional styles. . . . Certainly the design
is closer to Baskerville . . . than to the so-called classic romans
of Bodoni and Didot." One of Bell's most notable features is
its tapered serifs, in radical contrast to the bracketed serifs of
then-current English types, or to the European types John Bell
studied. ❡ The types were quite popular in the United States
in the early nineteenth century, but they were swiftly over-
shadowed by types based on Austin's later designs, that is, the
"Scotch" romans of the early 1800s. Bell began to return to
favor toward the end of the nineteenth century, appearing in
the work of influential American designers like D. B. Updike
and Bruce Rogers — despite only being available for hand composition. It was only in 1930 that the types were finally cut for
machine composition by the Monotype Corporation under
Morison's direction, ensuring that this handsome face
would be available for general book work and
guaranteeing its continued popularity.

DESIGN AND COMPOSITION BY CARL W. SCARBROUGH